Green Teaching

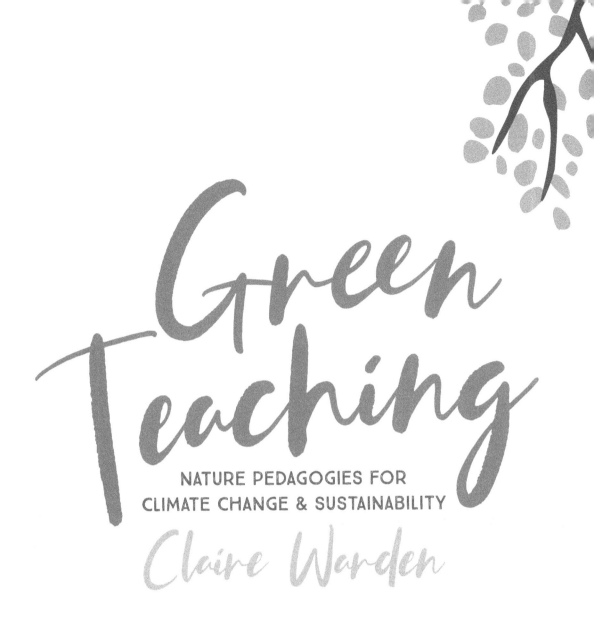

Green Teaching

NATURE PEDAGOGIES FOR CLIMATE CHANGE & SUSTAINABILITY

Claire Warden

CORWIN

Corwin
A SAGE company
2455 Teller Road
Thousand Oaks, California 91320
(800)233-9936
www.corwin.com

SAGE Publications Ltd
1 Oliver's Yard
55 City Road
London EC1Y 1SP

SAGE Publications India Pvt Ltd
B 1/I 1 Mohan Cooperative Industrial Area
Mathura Road
New Delhi 110 044

SAGE Publications Asia-Pacific Pte Ltd
3 Church Street
#10-04 Samsung Hub
Singapore 049483

Editor: Delayna Spencer
Assistant editor: Catriona McMullen
Production editor: Martin Fox
Copyeditor: Salia Nessa
Proofreader: Leigh Smithson
Indexer: Judith Lavender
Marketing manager: Dilhara Attygalle
Cover design: Wendy Scott
Typeset by: C&M Digitals (P) Ltd, Chennai, India

Library of Congress Control Number: 2021948354

British Library Cataloguing in Publication data

A catalogue record for this book is available from
the British Library

ISBN 978-1-5297-5218-2
ISBN 978-1-5297-5217-5 (pbk)

For family X

Contents

About the author

Claire Warden's approach to nature-based, child-led pedagogies has earned her international recognition as a pioneer in educational thinking. She is a multiple award-winning author with over 15 books to her credit. The sister book to this title called *Learning with Nature – Embedding Outdoor Practice* (Sage, 2015) is an essential text for understanding how to achieve quality in outdoor play and learning.

Claire has been recognised for her original contribution in the field of education, her thesis *The Creation and Theorisation of Nature Pedagogy*, and was awarded her PhD in 2019. Her inspirational research and approach to experiential learning has developed through a variety of experiences, including primary teaching, advisory work, lecturing in further education and development of the award winning Auchlone Nature Kindergarten in Scotland. She was awarded an international award of Exceptional Master Leader for her work on participatory planning through the Floorbooks® approach. The collaboration achieved through Floorbooks® places the voice of the child within the natural world. These two aspects are at the heart of planning, thus creating a respectful, inquiry-led relationship.

Claire works with governments and associations around the world to create high-quality, nature-based models of education, learning with nature inside, outside and beyond. Her philanthropic work includes international advisor to the Children and Nature Network, the World Forum Foundation and the International School Grounds Group, and she is the founder of Living Classrooms Community Interest Company (CIC), which runs the Virtual Nature School and the International Association of Nature Pedagogy.

Acknowledgements

Thank you to all those people who have inspired me through their legacy, to those who have shared in this journey with me and to those in the future who will carry on the commitment to nature pedagogy as a way of being inside, outside and beyond.

Illustrations (Figure 3.3, Figure 4.8, Figure 5.1, Figure 5.3, Figure 5.4, Figure 6.1, Figure 6.2, Figure 6.3, Figure 6.4, Figure 7.1, Figure 7.2, Figure 7.3 and Figure 7.4): Ann Shalovinskaya

Kinship graphic (Figure 6.5): Lara Warden

Case studies: The team at Auchlone Nature Kindergarten

Map of Auchlone Nature Kindergarten (Figure 2.4): Amy Cresswell

Shutterstock images (Figure 0.1, Figure 0.2, Figure 1.1, Figure 1.2, Figure 1.3, Figure 2.1, Figure 2.2, Figure 2.7, Figure 3.2, Figure 3.8, Figure 3.9, Figure 3.10, Figure 4.2, Figure 4.3, Figure 4.4 and Figure 4.7)

Introduction

Welcome to the world of nature pedagogy, a pedagogical approach that seeks to respect and support the rights of children and the planet with dual importance.

This book explores nature pedagogy and shows its impact on practice to share a transformation that offers an educational contribution to the increasingly urgent issues around the sustainability of humans and the needs of the planet we are on.

Figure 0.1 Size and scale

The size and scale of the issues we face require radical innovation in all aspects of the way we live. This book focuses on creating a societal shift in our perception of the role of the natural world in the education of humans. It does not solve all aspects of global climate change and distribution of food and water, but offers a perspective that is within reach for every educator in the world, every day.

The title of this book, *Green Teaching: Nature Pedagogies for Climate Change & Sustainability*, describes the need for educational change or perhaps affirmation to those educators who already support ecocentric teaching methods. Teaching as discussed in this book is not didactic, but it represents a skill in how to engage, care and educate children.

The words that often come to mind when you mention nature-based thinking are around awe and wonder, but let us not over romanticise the *other than human* aspects of nature. It is not a panacea, a solution for every ailment, issue and condition that humans have; it is not always cuddly and protective. It can be harsh, unyielding and honest, which for many humans makes it a threat to be controlled.

When we go into nature, it has the potential to offer a form of solace and a sense of wellbeing; when we learn about it, we are often humbled by the complexity and variety; when we learn with nature, it offers us intellectual provocations and solutions to many situations, from pain relief to engineering ideas. It is hoped that through all these aspects we can begin to do things that benefit humans and the planet, or indeed just for the planet.

The Earth is constantly changing, and those loose objects we play with outside such as sticks and stones are all on a journey alongside us as human beings. The pebble that children hold was once part of a mountain or under the sea; it was rock, a stone, now it's a pebble, but it will become a fragment, a grain, particles and molecules, and as such, will be recombined in other biological and chemical processes. We are part of this constant journey where a human lifetime is nothing more than a speck of time and all the decisions we make need to be made with the benefit of future generations in mind.

Figure 0.2 What kind of ancestor will you be?

As educators, teachers, pedagogues, parents, we need to ask the question: What kind of planet will we leave for our children? Will it be one where they will look back at the actions we take and feel proud of the wise choices of their ancestors?

This in turn asks us to consider what kind of children will we leave for the planet? How will we help them make wise choices in their lifetimes as they find themselves surrounded by an increasingly technological world?

It is also an interesting challenge to write a book that I have been thinking about my whole life, to know when to stop or indeed where to start, so I have started with a positive reminder of why what we do matters.

Each chapter provides imagery, stories and experiences in case studies and research to create a bridge from theory into practice. This process of thinking has created a framework of principles for a way of working, a pedagogical approach to care and education in the 21st century, built on a foundation of ancient ways of being. It includes visual mind maps that allow the reader to see the complexity of a curriculum and the interrelated nature of holistic learning with nature that arise when we plan for possibilities and not certainties.

In Chapter 1, we explore the reason why we need to consider exploring nature pedagogy rather than outdoor play in isolation.

Chapter 2 shares a definition to help understand the impact that we could have every day.

Chapter 3 pushes us to think more about the term *nature*. What do we mean and what impact does it then have on our day-to-day actions?

Chapter 4 investigates the idea of relationships, not just with humans but also with the rest of the natural world so we can reflect on how this changes our day-to-day choices.

Chapter 5 shares the principles of nature pedagogy and how they emerged from people who are fully immersed in the natural world every day, all day.

Chapter 6 offers a sustainable approach to care and education that places importance on the moments all of us have every day wherever we live and work.

Chapter 7 shares the implications for our practice so that everyone can do something to put the natural world at the heart of their pedagogy.

I hope this book supports you to place the needs of the natural world at the heart of the decisions that you make every day – from the environments you offer children to the style of planning for play and learning. It invites you to do what you can to create balance, and through that, achieve long-term sustainability.

One

Why do we need nature pedagogy?

Chapter overview

In a world that is full of definitions, this chapter explores why we need to consider another way of approaching how we work with children (our pedagogy) so that it becomes nature- or ecocentric. The list of terms linked to this field are wide and varied. We hear about outdoor play, environmental education, education for sustainability, nature play, nature-based practice and now nature pedagogy. Where then do we place the pedagogical practices that support children who view nature as a challenge to survival, or children whose confidence in their identity is interwoven with it? The drive that sits around care and education is the need to do something, to make a difference, but how do we do that in a way that we do not dominate the culture of the child and family, that is respectful of the variety and complexity of all of us? This chapter shares the global educational context and considers why we need to embrace nature pedagogy and not outdoor play in isolation.

Moments or 'rifts' (Caputo, 1987) exist in our lived experiences that offer us the opportunity to make connections from inside ourselves, outside into a relational ontology within society and into the beyond, as we interrelate with observable and unobservable phenomena. The desire to embrace the rifts and accept discord is an integral part of researching our practice as it allows us to consider patterns that exist between humans and the rest of the natural world.

This pedagogy uses three contexts of inside, outside and beyond (Warden, 2015, 2018). One interpretation of these contexts is as spatial locations; as spaces inside buildings, outside in landscaped areas and beyond boundary fences to nature presented on its own terms. A second interpretation is spiritual and emotional; from inside ourselves in a relationship with the natural world, to how this is then shared outside in society as a manifestation of values, to beyond into an unobservable connection we all have as humans to everything else we share on the planet.

Figure 1.1   Unobservable sense of connection

Sustainability as an approach to care and education

We need to change the way we live, which includes our approach to education and work. The whole of the natural world, including humans, is affected by the decisions that we make every day. These decisions are explored in Chapter 6 and their collective impact considered. Sustainability is a key issue that is affecting the balance of the Earth's systems and has accelerated climate change to the point that adaptation through evolution is impossible for some of the species on the planet; resource depletion and waste disposal are pressing issues and we have caused irreversible damage to ecosystems (Friedman, 2008). This has led to comments that this present period is the sixth major extinction period (Diamond, 1987) and is driving many people to take positive action.

Figure 1.2   Understand the facts and fiction

The issue sits in a collective space that needs to be taken seriously by society because the same messages are coming from all over the world. The humans are struggling. We are trying to sever our link to the natural world, which is an unattainable task. The desire to lead a predominantly sedentary life inside, to focus on immersive indoor technology of gaming, is changing our perceptions so that we experience nature in a created, second-hand world. The rise of digital pets is a result of the desire to want companionship but not relationship.

Figure 1.3   Entering the digital age

Perceptions of the natural world

During 2020, in the global pandemic, whilst working with educators to mentor them to support children and families to be outdoors, a range of views emerged. What came from that anecdotal research was that people seemed to align with three camps. The first was that 'nature' was threatening and was the reason for the Covid-19 virus and therefore everything connected to nature was cleaned or rejected; the next was that nature was a place to find solace and comfort; and the last was that being outside was going to be integral to the new normal. The words they shared in Table 1.1 offer a sense of hope that people see and feel the value of being outside, under the sky.

Table 1.1   The natural world as threat, solace and solution

Nature as a threat	Nature as solace	Nature as the solution
The cause of Covid-19	Peace	Future
Threat	Beauty	Joy
Disease	Solace	Sustainability
Virus	A new soundscape	Green
Attack	Escape	Provider
Death	Exercise	Care
Fear	Security	Protection
Hunger	Comfort	Balance
Harm	Reduced hazard	Hope
	Wellbeing	

Just as with the other animals we share the planet with, Kuo (2010) suggests that when we are put into environments that do not meet our physical, psychological and social needs, we will struggle to grow in a healthy way. The enforced lockdown in 2020 had a global impact, but has actually been happening more and more to the lives of children as their freedom to play outside in the local area has been reduced.

One way that we can make a difference is global awareness and understanding of the issues within education so that we can develop the skills we need to help the rest of the natural world and make wiser decisions for ourselves as a species. An area that offers a positive solution is pedagogy, as ecocentric interactions with children and families occur every day.

This book shares a nature pedagogy built on a history of environmental education and education for sustainability, but also respectfully acknowledges First Nation thinking. This suggests that the issue lies in a fundamental, deep-rooted belief of a human sense of privilege and power, and that we master the other aspects of the natural world, which builds a sense that we sit aside from nature and beyond its impact.

The global pandemic in 2020 caused people internationally to stop and think. The virus affected everyone, including those with wealth. Everyone felt a degree of vulnerability and exposure. The hope is that the visceral sense of loss from not being able to go outside, or the emotional relief we get when we do, is enough to remind us to make decisions that support an interdependent biological community.

Embracing ecocentric values in nature pedagogy will influence the next generation. Through two years of research, nine aspects of practice emerged (Warden, 2018) in an early year's environment in Scotland. These reflected the changing perspective of learning about being with the natural world inside, outside and beyond, so that the setting put nature at the heart of its decisions. It went beyond the ecological practices of litter management, power use and ethically sourced materials to a place where it was a way of being with children that accepted the observable loose materials, such as leaves, sticks and stones, and the unobservable phenomena that occurs when we feel emotionally connected to a place. In Chapter 5, we share how these went on to influence the 13 core principles of this nature pedagogy.

Given that not everyone lives in a place that they are from or wish to be in, we need to consider the practical challenges of access to the natural world and the impact of poverty on accessibility. Trees are often presented as icons to symbolise the work of both hereditary, linear connections and the value of the

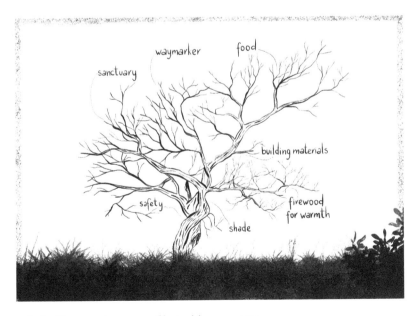

Figure 1.4 Perspectives are affected by poverty

natural world. There are, however, different views on that symbolism. Linear relationships may be a Western concept, and as discussed in Chapter 3, constitute one of several perspectives. A tree is full of play affordance (Nicholson, 1977) – it provides loose parts such as leaves and sticks. However, poverty changes our view of the tree, and we need to ask ourselves whether all children in the world view the natural world as full of wonder, or rather view it as a means of survival.

In some models of early education, the development of skills such as lighting fires or foraging is integrated into the programme. Although enjoyable, they are rather tokenistic compared to those experiences of children in parts of the world who need them for survival.

Poverty doesn't reside in one country; it resides in some form in all of them. Consider the experiences of children in incarceration, not only within a prison system, but in outdoor spaces that are sterile and unstimulating. Spare a moment to adopt the view of a child in war-torn environments when going outside can be about life and death. Every child on the planet has the right to play outside in the natural world, and until that goal is met, we all need to be advocates of a relational way of working.

Although much research supports the increase in the benefits of being outside under the sky, just looking at the natural world in a vicarious way inside can also be of benefit. In a study, Brown et al. (2013) showed images of more plant- and animal-based nature and images of urban spaces, and found that by viewing nature scenes there was a positive effect on the recovery of automatic function following acute mental stress.

This pedagogy offers a way of caring and teaching that supports human flourishing and acknowledges our relationship with the rest of the natural world. It is suggested that ecological sustainability is caught as well as taught (Miller and Spoolman, 2013; Schmidtz and Williott, 2002), but perhaps ecological sustainability is a re-awakening of our own thinking (rather than caught from someone else). This happens through the day-to-day moments that emerge from a settings ethos or culture, which needs to a be a conscious decision.

Nature pedagogies need to be an element of the way forward to sustaining the human population into the 21st century. Understanding the interrelationship between humans and the planet has never been clearer than now; however, the development of a sense of agency, empowerment and activism can be diverted or even suppressed through how children are educated.

We can all make a difference in the small choices we make every day; we can all make wise, ecocentric choices. If we can combine a cultural shift with the support for strategic sustainability goals, there will be an impact on us and the planet on which we live. Including the care and education of children in the solution acknowledges that we can help children and families care for and respect the other elements of the natural world. It can also go further than this in that it can create a culture of agency and activism to do something, to take action rather than embrace apathy.

Reframing our thinking through the transformation of education is within reach of all of us. We have learned *about* nature for centuries, studying it as if it sits aside from us as humans; we learn *in* it by going outside into it, but perhaps we need to really focus on making decisions *for* the natural world. In order to do that, I suggest that we need to learn *with* it so that we begin to understand our interrelationship. After all, how can we truly understand the melting of a glacier if we haven't felt the coldness of ice in our hands? When you feel the effect of heat on ice and see it melting away before your eyes, you have a deep-level awareness and understanding of your impact that you can build on in the future. Children exploring the elements of earth, fire, water and air provide myriad moments every day that will offer them the chance to know and love the natural world, and in turn, feel the agency to make a difference.

CONSIDER

How are the aspects of your practice connected into a defined pedagogy?

What has influenced your thinking as a professional?

What are the ways that you could become more active in helping colleagues become aware of the need for ecocentric practices?

Understanding the issues that we face as global professionals

The 2020 pandemic has made a difference to societies around the world, as people had a glimpse of what could be – large cities with no pollution, animals back in parkland and the value of our freedom to be outside with people we care for. An opportunity for transformation is possible through a societal shift, or what Caputo (1987) refers to as a rift in thinking. When we embrace times of disequilibrium and disharmony, they urge us to see formally unseen patterns, connections or aspects of our work that we are unaware of. This is an opportunity for rapid human change across the planet that has never been experienced before in history.

Education is situated and influenced by a number of factors such as law, politics, culture and economics (Warden, 2015). All of the work we do as advocates for children's rights is set within a period of time, so that we build on the work that has been done before and leave a legacy that can be built on into the future. The direction we take in our pedagogy therefore has a multi-generational impact.

Within the context that we work, there are several aspects of success in relation to the national policy here in Scotland. The drive began over 30 years ago with individual campaigners, which then moved into starting up independent settings such as Auchlone Nature Kindergarten so that people could visit and feel a more immersive model in practice. Now, outdoor play and education for sustainability is embedded in national policy, the quality inspection process, and supports value-based models practice with children and families. It is acknowledged as important from government to educators. However, there is still a journey to take as we move away from the learning in and about the natural world to learning with and ultimately for it. There is always space to build up professional agency through skill development and knowledge of the natural world *and* how to be in it with children.

We have more visual awareness of the diversity of animals and plants on the Earth, but we appear to lack the foundational knowledge of their role in the ecosystem, their name or their requirements for habitat.

This media-driven awareness has brought together inspirational groups of young people who want to make a difference; however, the tension is that the knowledge we gather is not through direct experience or engagement in real world learning, 'this knowledge is rather rigid and full of erroneous interpretation and models' (Rickinson, 2001: 220). In early education, this means that we need to give time to understanding and acquiring knowledge of the natural world for ourselves, but also how to be sensitive to the invitations to engage that it affords children.

Having the responsibility of being the guide or facilitator we carry two roles, that of the holder of memories and also the person who makes the links and connections to the motivations of children. These are some of the skills within nature pedagogy. They are explored further in Chapter 7 in the implications for practice.

Western understanding and presentation of the issues have dominated the media and our perception of the issues. In an equitable world, everyone has a right to be heard and many conversations we have around sustainability would be more respectful and culturally sensitive if they were with Indigenous elders, researchers and authors.

As professionals across the world, we encounter the natural world in a wide variety of ways. In conversation with colleagues in the leadership team of the Nature Action Collaborative for Children (NACC) of the World Forum, we spoke of the bias of only having a single viewpoint, conveying a single story and how we can achieve so much more as a global collaborative.

Raed from Jordan (personal communication, 2021) writes:

We still face a lack of environmental education programs targeting children at an early age. I believe this work on nature pedagogy will highlight the practical experience for children connecting children with nature in parallel with the theoretical part of child development. It is important today to help the children learn with enjoyment and understand the value of nature wherever they are in the world.

This is just one voice and perspective from millions around the world. Each has value and enriches our work so that we consider our professional collective impact.

This chapter is the foundation for this book through stating why we need to change the way we work with children from merely being outside to developing our skills and knowledge in the field of nature pedagogy. The rest of the book will take a series of key points in turn and explore them in more detail to give practical advice on how to develop nature pedagogy and use it every day. The next chapter starts this process by exploring a definition of nature pedagogy and explores how this pedagogy creates a value-based framework for the way that we live and work with young children.

SUMMARY

- There is an urgent need to create balance between human need and the rest of the planet.
- Human perception of the natural world can be affected by their current and past experiences.
- A sustainable approach to education and care needs to include *how* we integrate nature into our pedagogy.
- Everyone can make a difference – small everyday choices and national strategic goals will both have an impact.

Two

Nature pedagogy - a definition

Chapter overview

This chapter shares the journey that defines nature pedagogy as the art of being with nature across the three locations of inside, outside and beyond, but also explores the use of inside, outside and beyond to explore inside ourselves, outside with others in our close community and beyond as a global community of professionals.

The complexity of nature pedagogy cannot be reduced to a single model of education, but rather it is a way of working with children that acknowledges pedagogy as value driven. It is not something to be studied alone, but is a practice that is built on relationships. This chapter details the research that sits beneath this nature pedagogy and places it in the wider context of outdoor play.

The vision of a sustainable nature-based pedagogy

Winston Churchill stated, 'we shape our buildings and afterwards our buildings shape us' (Churchill, 1943). As the buildings have shaped us, we have become progressively removed from the natural world. Our lives are full of moments where we are pushed to reconsider our relationship with each other and the wider world.

The moments that Caputo (1987) describes as 'rifts' allow connections to occur in our lived experiences. It was through these moments that I developed a deeper sense of the interrelated nature of life that embraces the living and the non-living as being in a state of constant flux and movement. It is this sense of spirituality, rather than religion, that is explored through the complexities of understanding educational practice through the unobservable world of quantum science. Caputo, as a postmodernist thinker, embraces the uncertainty of human existence when he states:

> I do not think that anyone ever really succeeds in getting to one side or the other of this undecidable rift, that no-one is or is not religious … If we face the cold truth … we do not know who we are, not if we are honest. (Caputo, 1987: 287–8)

Ellsworth suggests that these 'moments' in our lives are significant:

> What is it, then, to sense one's self in the midst of learning as experience, in the moment of learning, in the presence of a coming knowing, in this interleaving of cognition and sensation/movement? (Ellsworth, 2005: 149)

As outdoor practitioners, we respond to the unexpected and unpredictable in the natural world. Moving our thinking from more adult-generated ideas of things to do outside to explore the skills and possibilities of nature pedagogy inside, outside and beyond is a step towards enhanced sustainability in education.

Existing work on outdoor play and learning

This book is focused on the observable and unobservable relationships that humans have with both the living and non-living elements of the natural world. This aspect of practice sits within a larger body of work on outdoor play and learning, but it seeks to challenge some aspects of what we think that is and offers a framework to aid the understanding of the range of ways that nature-based outdoor play and learning is experienced (Chapter 4). Nature pedagogy is defined as a value-driven, pedagogical approach that sits beneath all these experiences and models of nature-based education. A continuum is created by considering to what extent nature pedagogy, as defined in this book, is integrated into early years practice. It starts with holistic Indigenous pedagogies of constant contact, moves through short duration, nature-based models such as forest school, to no physical access to being outside in the natural world.

This book expands on what is viewed as the current work around nature-based practice in an effort to be more inclusive. The written materials have grown from a Western, largely Nordic foundation of nature-based practice. The engagement with nature as 'an individual's subjective sense of their relationship with the natural world' (Waite et al., 2016: 52) is a relatively recent focus in Western, environmental discourse. However, it is not a new concept, and as shown later in this chapter, it stretches back to Rousseau (1762/2003) in the West and is a way of being in numerous, First Nation cultures around the world.

Many studies (Chawla, 1998; Wells and Lekies, 2006; Wilson, 1997) support children's engagement with the natural world as developing concern for the environment, but there is new research (Sandell and Öhman, 2013) that suggests that just being in nature is not enough to consolidate environmental positivism. The adult, or nature pedagogue in my work, has a role to play in supporting children in nature-based pedagogies. The adult understanding of the human–nature relationship was viewed as a simplistic understanding by Chawla and Cushing (2007), which in turn affects the quality and depth of awareness. The situation of the child, affected by facets of politics and cultural world view, is indeed complex, and like Taylor (2013) and her concept of 'common worlds', Chawla and Cushing (2007) seek to ask complicated questions of the human–nature relationship. This book aims to support this understanding through challenging the adult awareness of the unobservable world and, through that process, deepen understanding of nature pedagogy.

Within this educational work there is little research that explores unobservable moments of being with nature, as examined in Chapter 4. The most recent research that exists to the best of my knowledge explores the place of the development of spirit and a love of life (Lee-Hammond and Colliver, 2017), and spirit and journey-making (Jannok Nutti, 2017). This book explores the unobservable sense of being with the natural world in a relational pedagogy that embraces a 'totality of relations' (French, 1986: 542) and how it manifests itself in practice.

To date, much of the research around nature immersion models, such as nature kindergartens or outdoor nurseries, looks to Nordic research and not to Indigenous pedagogies (Warden, 2017). On examination of a list of seven significant points from a research review of outdoor learning, not just nature-based practice, there are obvious gaps in this process, as discussed in Chapter 4.

The comprehensive international review was collated by editors Waller et al. (2017) and states that what we can say about outdoor learning is that:

- There is a strong relationship between time spent outside in natural environments, positive wellbeing, increased happiness and better mental health (Bragg, 2013; Capaldi et al., 2014; Gill, 2014; Richardson et al., 2016; Wolsko and Lindberg, 2013).
- There is a strong link between exercise in natural wild places and general wellbeing (Askwith, 2014; Aspinall et al., 2013; Mitchell, 2013).
- The overall positive health effects of increased, risky, outdoor play provide greater benefit than the health effects associated with avoiding outdoor risky play (Brussoni et al., 2015; Little et al., 2012; MacQuarrie et al., 2015; Sandseter, 2012).
- Children and young people experience outdoor environments as places of meaning and significance (Mawson, 2014; Tovey, 2007; Waite and Pratt, 2011; Waters and Maynard, 2010).
- Outdoor play supports social interaction and helps to nurture emotional understanding (Perrin and Benassi, 2009; Waite et al., 2013; Yeh et al., 2015).
- There is a relatively strong relationship between time spent outside in natural environments and environmental awareness, nature relatedness and positive approaches to sustainability (Ärlemalm-Hagsér, 2013; Davis, 2010; Gurholt, 2014; Jóhannesson et al., 2011).
- Regular outdoor experiences include benefits for learning, motivation and achievement at school (Fagerstam, 2012; Hill and Brown, 2014; Szczepanski and Dahlgren, 2011).

The research is collated to give a broad range of perspectives, but this field is challenged by its position as being from academic thinkers who have world views and perspectives that may be biased – not from intent but from the world view they hold.

The examples above demonstrate a growing amount of research, but highlight two things of note. The first is the 'almost total absence of Indigenous researcher voices' (Waller et al., 2017: 8). Only four chapters (Lee-Hammond and Colliver, 2017: 318; Nutti, 2017: 333; Rowan, 2017: 395; Warden, 2017: 279) out of 40 had any direct connection to Indigenous researchers. It is important that we consider whether there is a subjugation of both the natural world and Indigenous peoples through a lack of attention to Indigenous research methodologies by Indigenous researchers in Western academic publications.

The second aspect is the bias in the countries and cultures represented. Research on outdoor play and learning from Asia, Africa and South America was identified by Waller et al. (2017) as being lacking. Finally, Waller et al. state that 'to date, research in outdoor play and learning has not deeply explored the inter-actions of children and young people in nature at the spiritual level' (2017: 8). The chapter on nature pedagogy (Warden, 2017) in the *SAGE Handbook of*

Outdoor Play and Learning (Waller et al., 2017) was one of only three which did this, and indeed the only one to research the practitioner's connection to the unobservable phenomena that the Auchlone Nature Kindergarten team refer to as 'sustaining the Auchlone spirit' (Warden, 2017: 285). It is therefore in this space that this thinking resides, bringing together the notion of interrelated perspectives and educational practice to explore a sense of being with nature in a way that could be described as more than human, unobservable and spiritual.

Nature's child

This overview demonstrates the need for further work in the field of the unobservable elements of our human relatedness to the natural world. A leading contemporary exponent of children's special relations to nature, Chawla (2002), unashamedly reclaims Romantic traditions to explore these moments of awe and wonder that for her cannot be explained by cognitive theories.

She suggests that their significance exceeds the limits of rational consciousness and that they not only momentarily connect children to something beyond themselves, but that this sense of connection stays with them into adulthood. Further, she maintains that there are mythical and magical dimensions to these childhood experiences, which she describes as taking place in 'ecstatic places and functioning as radioactive jewels buried within us, emitting energy across the years of our life' (Chawla, 1990: 18). Her focus has been to find 'different ways of knowing nature in childhood, as well as different ways of relating childhood to adulthood' (Chawla, 2002: 200).

Within this definition, nature pedagogy seeks to create a pedagogy of relational power balance between humans and the rest of their natural world. We reside on the land, but we influence everything on the planet, so we need to make decisions for the seen and unseen aspects. It was Rousseau (1762) who suggested that children were superior to adults in their connection to nature, suggesting that it was other to and better than the way that adults engage. This reiterates some of Sobel's (2008) work where he suggests that there are windows of sensitivity that exist in childhood. However, the idea that there are windows that close completely as human beings, as participants, is questionable as we cannot be closed from the natural system that allows us to live.

The second aspect noted by Rousseau was the idea of 'negative education' (Rosseau, 2003: 59), which originated with Rousseau's desire to protect and ringfence time for children to learn 'in *their* own time, within nature' (Rosseau, 2003: 58) without the education of adults. This is as true today as it was in the 18th century, as we observe didactic, reductionist strategies being introduced into the early years sector in the form of over-directed nature experiences or unconnected activity-based planning.

Rousseau stated that a child:

> Receives his lessons from Nature ... learns the more rapidly . . . his body
> and his mind are called into exercise at the same time. Acting always in
> accordance with his own thought, and not according to that of another,
> he is continually uniting two processes, the stronger and the more robust
> he becomes. (Rosseau, 2003: 86)

It is reflected in the approach of seeing silence and stillness as a place of complexity, rather than a lack of knowledge or interest. The place of a silent pedagogy was explored in Ollin's (2008) work as being the conscious choice on the part of an adult to abstain from verbal interventions.

There is a greater alignment here with Dewey's (1980) work, in his proposal that, building on Rousseau's ideas, he extends the concept of the child acting on his own will to combine the need to both explore his own thinking, that is situated in experience, and develop the relationship with the role and interaction of the adult.

The third aspect of Rousseau's work that is significant with respect to this writing is his view of nature as an external and material world in which we live, that was other than man. Furthermore, a link can be established from the work of Rousseau, through the work of Johan Pestalozzi (the Swiss pedagogue and educational reformer), to the work of Froebel. Pestalozzi had been fascinated by Rousseau's work and spent considerable time exploring his philosophies and working to extend them. Froebel, although born in Germany, worked for a time in Switzerland with Pestalozzi and was introduced to and influenced by the work of Rousseau.

Rousseau wanted to support the 'education of things' (Rosseau, 2003: 2) that were primarily natural. Froebel extended this into the method of nature, but unlike Rousseau he had a background in mineralogy and scientific study, which led him to suggest that there were infallible natural laws. It is interesting to consider the seminal work of Isaac Newton, who, although widely considered as a scientist and mathematician, was both deeply religious and a philosopher fascinated by the natural world. He believed that rational laws applied to all processes within the universe, but also that the continuance of those processes, and therefore nature itself, was an act of God.

Quantum science is the study of the smallest possible units of anything (for example matter or energy), and we can conceivably extend Newton's philosophical position in the light of modern quantum science by considering the potential for it to demonstrably prove the physical basis for Newton's laws and beliefs (see Chapter 3).

Rousseau and Froebel (their ideas and philosophies) are commonly used as the rationale for the use of hands-on learning equipment, rather than in the support of nature-based, negative education, which is rooted in spirituality and the drive to be closer to the ultimate deity.

Brosterman states that Froebel's philosophy guides adults to understand that they should be actively:

> . . . embracing the spiritual potential within a person, relations between people in a free society, the place of the individual in relation to the nature that surrounds and includes him, and the [divine and natural] life force that controls growth in all things. (Brosterman, 2002: 3)

However, Taylor suggests that education that was faithful to the method of nature and revealed 'the divine essence of things' (Taylor, 2013: 40) was in fact a way of manifesting Rousseau's philosophy of unity and was intended to lead man towards enlightenment. This diverges from nature pedagogy in its search for unity with a single deity. If there is a principal motive in supporting the growth of nature pedagogy, it is to see balance between living and non-living worlds in a form of being with nature that engages us in mind, body and spirit in a sustainable way (see Chapter 5).

Scientific rationalism (Fuchs, 2004) took hold of Western secular schooling as rational pedgagogical naturalism. With an emphasis on scientific rationalism and a natural pedagogy rooted in the earth sciences, schools adhering to Maria Montessori's thinking flourished (Whitescarver and Cossentino, 2008) and the creative pedagogies inherent in Waldorf Steiner schools spread across Europe (Uhrmacher, 1995). Our challenge is to create appreciation and balance across the models of education, such as Montessori centres, Steiner schools, forest schools, nature pre-schools, bush kinder outdoor nurseries, and so on, to promote collective conversations around nature pedagogy, not their points of difference or supremacy.

Montessori schools have emerged through Maria Montessori's 'fascination with natural phenomena' (Taylor, 2013: 44–5). She embraced the pedagogical cultivation of children's careful observations of the world around them so that they could become competent 'worshippers and interpreters of the spirit of nature' (Montessori, 1912, cited by Fuchs, 2004: 169). This careful observation led to adult-structured tasks and resources around nomenclature, species and geographical features that are still used today. However, Montessori did not support the pedagogy that children should be introduced to make believe and an unobservable world. Nature pedagogy can only really be embraced with an awareness of the unobservable as we develop the language of description and understanding through quantum thinking. The appearance and operation of models of nature-based practice emerge from their unique sense of place (Sobel, 2008) and therefore can embrace diversity of location and connection of interrelation. This understanding may be the way to develop more connective, supportive conversations between people, rather than an increasing separation between them due to market competition and a human drive to process. This concept is explored more comprehensively in Chapter 3.

An approach to learning *with* nature

The definition of a nature kindergarten is a 'a blend of three spaces' (Warden, 2007: 8): inside a shelter, outside in a natural play area and beyond the fence in wilder spaces. What these three spaces truly represent was explored in more depth in *Learning with Nature – Embedding Outdoor Practice* (Warden, 2015). The book used a process of using graphics called 'Diagrams of practice' to represent the three spaces to notice and feel connections in, about and with nature through the use of time, space, resources and the adult role. The use of diagrams and graphics allowed the presentation of more fluid thinking around the idea of 'learning *about* nature as a thing to study' (Warden, 2015: 29) rather than connect to or as 'learning *in* nature as being a location outside' (Warden, 2015: 30). The argument that is central to this book is that we learn *with* nature. In this way, when nature is presented in many different global models, most of which seek to define and differentiate themselves from the others, from outdoor areas to forest schools, we can connect through values that guide us towards changing pedagogy *for* the benefit of the ecosystem (that includes humans). Moving away from operational facets or observable features of one model takes us to conversations of inclusivity, where myriad ways of being with the natural world are embraced.

Kinship

Given that it is an integral part of the definition of nature pedagogy, as it embraces learning about, in, with and for the natural world, kinship is explained here in the context of this book. Ruth Wilson (2020) suggests that it is about experiencing kinship with nature all around us versus trying to connect with nature out there. A kinship perspective takes us beyond both science (Sideris, 2017) and stewardship (Taylor, 2017). There is detail surrounding this concept of kinship in Chapter 6 where we explore the work of the International Environmental Kinship (EKI).

Figure 2.1 Cultural tradition connected to place

Haraway (2016) describes kinship as *affinity, not identity.* The idea of kinship includes a blurring of the human and non-human, and the interdependence of us all on the planet.

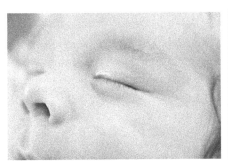

Figure 2.2 Interdependence and connection

Defining pedagogy

The use of the term 'pedagogy' warrants some clarification here. Pedagogy as used in the northern European tradition encompasses the everyday formal and informal practices of the education of children. In Greek, the literal translation is leading children, where *ped* represents child and *agogus* means leading. Andragogy is therefore the practice of leading man (*andr*), which when working with practitioners would appear to be more appropriate. This literal translation is slightly different from defining pedagogy as 'the method and practice of teaching' (Oxford English Dictionary, 2018), where there is no mention of the age of the student. The common usage of pedagogy in Europe has been one of nurturing learning.

Nature pedagogy could be as simple as a method of leading children in natural environments. However, in working alongside staff *with* nature, they describe pedagogy in a different, more creative and fluid way. A colleague, Gillian McAuliffe, describes it in this way:

> I like to think of it as a dance. It is a dance which engages curriculum, students, teachers, indoor classrooms, outdoor classrooms and the wild and built environments outside the school gate. This dance is characterised by the fluid nature of the choreography, with participants sometimes working together, sometimes separately, sometimes in small groups. The dance happens on the stage of life and engages those elements and the content which best supports the journey of the students and the stories they want to hear and tell. If the notion of the dance is understood, then the learning environments will be without walls and boundaries, and the integration you have identified is the natural and only way to go. (Warden, 2015: 32)

This book shares the idea that although pedagogy is a relationship-based dynamic, which describes the interaction between the learner and the pedagogue, allowing the social context, complete with histories, hierarchies, customs, teleologies and narratives to intertwine (Kamler and Thompson, 2006), it is also a felt, unobservable spirit within humans that we can embrace in our work with the natural world.

The word 'pedagogy' is derived from the Greek language, as noted earlier. In Greek society there were, however, two clear expectations of the role of people in relation to the education of children. Pedagogues were perceived as companions to the development of the whole child (*paidagögus*), whilst subject teachers (*didáskalos*) were focused on knowledge.

Plato talks about pedagogues as 'men who by age and experience are qualified to serve as both leaders (*hëgemonas*) and custodians (*paidagögous*)' of children, which was cited by Longenecker (1982: 53), with no reference to a relational artistry, but rather a science of knowledge to be studied.

The debate around whether pedagogy is the same as the didactic methods to which the Greeks referred can be noted throughout history. Immanuel Kant wrote a book called *On Pedagogy* (*Über Pädagogik*), in which he stated:

> Education includes the nurture of the child and, as it grows, its culture. The latter is firstly negative, consisting of discipline, that is, merely the correcting of faults. Secondly, culture is positive, consisting of instruction

and guidance (and thus forming part of education). Guidance means directing the pupil in putting into practice what he has been taught. Hence the difference between a private teacher who merely instructs, and a tutor or governor who guides and directs his pupil. The one trains for school only, the other for life. (Kant, 1900: 23–4)

In 1648, Comenius wrote *The Great Didactic*. As Gundem states, it suggested that 'the fundamental aims of education generate the basic principle of Didactica Magna, omnis, omnia, omnino – to teach everything to everybody thoroughly, in the best possible way' (1992: 53).

The separation of the activity of 'teaching' from the activity of defining 'what is taught' was put forward by Hamilton (1999: 139). In continental Europe, this led to a growing discussion of the process of teaching, in contrast to the didactics of guidance and knowledge. Gundem (1992) suggests that Comenius believed that every human being should strive for perfection in all that is fundamental for life and do this as thoroughly as possible. Comenius stated, 'every person must strive to become (1) a rational being, (2) a person who can rule nature and him or herself, and (3) a being mirroring the creator' (Gundem, 1992: 53).

Although in terms of nature pedagogy, one could challenge the outcomes Comenius suggests we strive for, in terms of an emphasis on the rational above a creative/intuitive, the desire to rule nature rather than work as an integral part of it, and the emulation of a single creator, we need to place these within their historical context. His principles, as presented by Gundem, still have a resonance in conversations today when we discuss how to work with children:

Teaching must be in accordance with the student's stage of development.

All learning happens through the senses.

One should proceed from the specific to the general, from what is easy to the more difficult, from what is known to the unknown.

Teaching should not cover too many subjects or themes at the same time.

Teaching should proceed slowly and systematically – nature makes no jumps.

(Gundem, 1992: 54)

The last of these points has particular relevance to nature pedagogy, as the storied experience of life does move slowly and systematically within the telling when the natural world is the contextual framework for our narratives (Warden, 2017: 283).

Figure 2.3   Nature time – slow and long term

This perspective on the cultural placement of education was brought to the fore by Bruner when he suggested that teachers 'need to pay particular attention to the cultural contexts in which they are working and of the need to look at folk theories and folk pedagogies' (1996: 44–65). In the rise of nature-based experiences, we can see the increased number of children who are connecting to crafts that may have been more traditionally associated with folk craft, such as rope making, basket weaving and so on, which could be further explored in its connection to folk pedagogy as a route to greater clarity around being with nature. In the work of nature pedagogy, there is undoubtedly an influence from the continental traditions of social pedagogy, as presented by Lorenz (1994), Smith (2009) and Cameron (2004, 2011). In Scotland, we went as far as suggesting we should support the growth of a country-specific, culturally specific, Scottish pedagogue (Cohen, 2008) who would connect to the micro-narratives of people and place.

There are three points to consider in terms of didactics and the pedagogy suggested by Smith (2009): the first is the use of the term pedagogy, as it takes us back to the originality of the term to actively consider accompanying as a skill; secondly, that pedagogy 'involves significant helping and caring' (Smith, 2009: 10); and thirdly, that it is engaged in 'bringing learning to life' (Smith, 2009: 10).

All of these have direct relevance to a definition of nature pedagogy, in that to walk alongside someone is complex and skilful as it requires us to give up our dominance and power to be content in our role. 'The human in the pedagogue *allows* us to have spirit, in the passions that animate or move us, in the moral sense of the value, ideals and attitudes that guide us as beings, in the kind of person we want to be in the world' (Doyle and Smith, 1999: 33–4). When we develop this skill to be alongside children and develop nature pedagogy we can start to explore being with nature.

─────────────── **CONSIDER** ───────────────

To what extent is your pedagogy affected by your sense of being with nature?

Emergence of *being* with nature

Thinking takes time, and as practitioners we are constantly learning. The phrases 'There is a connection between the nurturing aspects of nature and human beings' and 'We have an underlying awareness of the need that children have for the fundamental aspects of being on the planet' (Warden, 2007: 6) suggest and share an awareness of engaging in nature-based outdoor learning for a need for being.

There is also a settling down, a calmer sense of being, a stronger connection to being in nature in a more synergistic way, perhaps even as a humble observer through writing in a more prosaic genre with references made to homely objects, such as carpets:

> Imagine a world where the lines were harsh and unyielding, the textures were consistent and variation is unheard of. Does it inspire you? Now imagine a place where the carpet changes every day, the ceiling is a myriad of different colours, light, shadow and movement. The feelings and movement completely surround you, sometimes breezy, sometimes cold, other times warm. Unexpected wonders fly, sometimes full of colour and sometimes full of noise and movement. If we really want children to thrive, we need to let their connection to nature nurture them. (Warden, 2007: back cover)

When children spend all day, every day, in a fully immersive space, they develop a sense of the variety and complexity of the natural world, as we see in this case study.

─────────────── **CASE STUDY** ───────────────

Mapping our place

The mapping process is part of an annual cycle of inquiry into our sense of being with nature and through this process we come to understand which areas of the site have significance to children rather than areas defined by adults. To support the conversations from the kindergarten to home, we share maps made by children but also have a map drawn by a member of the adult team, as shown below. Although parents and

(Continued)

families visit the site and spend time in it, having a map to look at together helps that process in the home but also in the wider community.

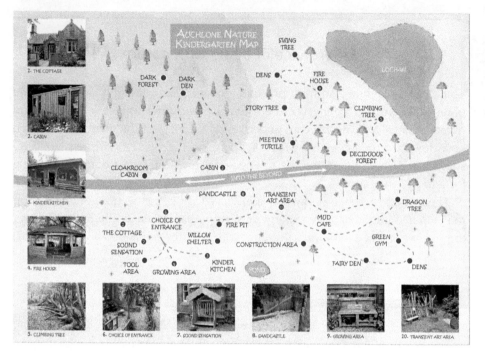

Figure 2.4 Auchlone map to share with children and families

Going beyond the gate, into the Dark Forest, to the Lochan, the Dragon Tree and the Fire House, is done as a whole group and naming has become part of the tradition of the site as children name areas of significance, such as the Meeting Turtle or the Story Tree. These names are passed down through groups of children, and over the past 14 years more and more have been added as the site evolves and more stories of children are woven into it. Children map out their own ideas as we can see in the map from home to here, a map of my place, and maps of the site and the journeys we take together as a community. There is a shift that happens when children go across locations; going beyond the gate is both physical and metaphorical as the group dynamic and the energy level change. On these journeys, the landscape around invites children to hesitate, to pause, to run towards, to climb as they read the invitations that the natural environment affords.

The map shared and their own maps are used to make decisions and plan routes and experiences that balance the needs of the children and the knowledge of the animals and plants that we share the site with. Areas are truly known by children through-out the year because they visit every day all year round: 'We don't go to where the pheasant's nesting because she needs quiet', or jump in the tadpole pools in the spring because 'they are just babies and they will die under my wellies.'

Empowerment of children and the agency to make decisions about where to go on the site is a skill acquired over time and not all children feel empathetic towards animals and plants.

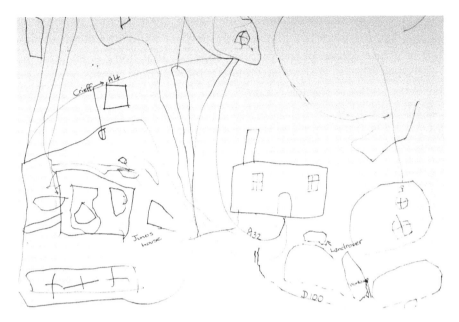

Figure 2.5   'My map from home to here'

The slowing down and awareness of place comes through the case study. It shows how the process of revisiting, through engaging with the environment, is dynamic and process led. It cannot really be achieved until there is a balance of child-led, adult-led and environment-led moments. Through the handling of natural, loose parts to make artefacts, there is a touching, a processing that can be seen from children's desires to explore blending, grinding and smoothing, in an almost anthropological way.

> Nature Pedagogy is a natural way of working *with* children that is all encompassing, from the educational environments we create, the process of assessment and planning, through to the learning journeys that we encourage children and families to take throughout childhood. (Warden, 2015: 14, emphasis added)

However, rather than being purely humancentric, we can explore the idea that 'being with nature' in a two-way, unobservable relationship with the tangible materials and the natural world itself is a more sustainable approach to living.

Indigenous pedagogies

'We're tired of trees', sigh Gilles Deleuze and Felix Guattari in a moment of exasperation, 'They've made us suffer too much' (Deleuze and Guattari,

2004: 17). The genealogical model of human ancestry and its linearity is challenged by the work of Deleuze and Guattari (2004). The dendritic model (often of a tree shown in the picture) suggests that there is an orderliness to our being human, that we are related only to those in the past and that the context and land (nature) on which we live and breathe has less impact on us than the genes we possess. Relational models explored by Deleuze and Guattari suggest we adopt a new paradigm for thinking that is likened to a rhizome.

Figure 2.6   Rhizome, dendritic and mycelium root systems

These analogies allow us to look at a more chaotic model of relationships, which are present within generational blocks of time. If we look to a mesh or a mycelium growth as an alternative to the genealogical model of human ancestry and its linearity, as Ingold (2000) suggests, we can visualise an interconnected mesh, which represents the interrelationships between the context of the land and those people we encounter in our lives. This aspect is explored fully in Chapter 3 prior to the consideration of the definitions of nature and being with nature in a relational way.

CONSIDER

How do you consider the interrelationship of people, place and environment?

Defining nature

When we think about the way we work in, learn about and learn with nature it broadens our understanding to be much more than outdoor play. Caring and educating young children across just three spaces; inside 'educational' buildings, outside in natural play spaces and beyond their boundary fences in wilder spaces, where children may encounter 'nature on nature's terms' (Warden, 2007) has placed outdoor play to become one aspect of a deeper nature-based pedagogy. The journeys, both physically and metaphorically, that children take over locations offer many points of difference that the natural environment affords.

The complex relationship that we encounter is touched upon by French, who builds upon the postmodern concept of nature as an 'almost incomprehensibly complex, open, interconnected totality of interrelationships' (French, 1986: 542–4). Relationships is a major theme in this book and is examined in Chapter 3 in terms of interconnectedness with nature.

Being with nature in a relational way

There is a need to look at alternative methodologies to support the human race beyond an anthropocentric view where the whole world revolves around human need, but in a 'partnership of mutual consideration' (Dodson, 2015). This book looks beyond the physical learning spaces and intellectual stimulation, to the more complex domains, to explore what Keeler (2008) refers to as 'food for the soul'.

Figure 2.7   Is this our legacy of the late 20th century?

There is evidence from artists such as Hanson (cited in Gablik, 1993: 301–309), in their work to photograph the toxic waste materials around nuclear sites, of their belief that the legacy of the late 20th century will be the disease of the planet, rather than positive icons of human achievement, such as the pyramids. Rather than objectifying the damaged and scarred nature of the planet (Kovel, 2002; Oliver, 2005), we need to understand its impact on all facets of our being (Oliver, 2009: 54).

In many countries over the past 40 years, children have spent increasingly limited time outside and may be losing their sensitivity to the natural world (Waller et al., 2017). In the UK, since the 1970s, the physical area that children roam freely over has decreased by almost 90 per cent (Moss, 2012). Moss goes on to support Louv's comment that children are effectively under 'well meaning, protective house arrest' (cited in Moss, 2012: 4). However, the assertion that screen time affects green time is an oversimplification. Studies by Waller and Tovey (2014) suggest that there can be a balance of outdoor and indoor experiences, but that this is culturally situated and, further, 'it is connected to socioeconomic status and other demographic factors, such as age or gender' (Waite et al., 2016: 1).

In the following chapter, we will explore definitions of nature so that we can come to a common understanding of how to use the term in this work on nature pedagogy and have a positive contribution to the long-term sustainability of the planet and us.

—————————————— **SUMMARY** ——————————————

- Pedagogies that work well with the natural world are consultative, co-constructed and focused on child-led inquiry.
- Nature pedagogy is about learning about, in, with and for the natural world.
- Nature pedagogy resonates with First Nation thinking and, as it focuses on the elements of fire, earth, air and water, can be used in our practice in urban and rural spaces.
- Nature pedagogy is the art of being with nature inside, outside and beyond as a physical location and a metaphor.

Three

What is nature?

Chapter overview

The word 'nature' is complex in its meaning, as it is used to describe both the physical world and a force or phenomenon. In this chapter, we consider whether it is a force or phenomenon of the metaphysical world that we feel but cannot touch. This chapter explores the concept that there is an interrelatedness between all parts of the natural world; that it is in constant movement, flux and adaptation; that it is living and non-living and concurrently observable and unobservable. When the definition of nature is clarified, it becomes more apparent that the values of nature pedagogy run beneath the many models of nature-based education, not all of which acknowledge the non-living and unobservable world.

There is gathering research evidence, as detailed in the Introduction, of the diminishing opportunities for children to have contact with the other aspects of the natural world beyond themselves. Children in urban spaces are even more disadvantaged, with a 2011 study (King's College, London, 2011) finding that in the UK:

- 1–3 million children never go anywhere that might include nature
- 40 per cent spend less time in nature than previously
- 10 per cent visit nature with school but only 5 per cent do so in deprived communities.

We need to clarify what we mean by nature. In the results above, we need to dig down to ascertain what the researchers defined nature as being, in order for us to be able to really understand the results.

CONSIDER

Does nature mean anything that is green, in which case, how do we view rock?

Is nature the world that we can see? If so, under the sea is not included.

Is nature an area of greenery that we have in mind? In which case, how much?

How do we classify the place of air, the breeze?

In this writing, nature is used to represent everything within and around us in an interconnected mesh. It is framed through principles in Chapter 5, sustainability in Chapter 6 and the four elements of earth, fire, air and water that we explore in Chapter 7. Within those four elements, we acknowledge that some aspects are seen like a leaf, but other aspects such as photosynthesis are unseen.

Nature pedagogy has become a way of being with nature that puts the natural world at the heart of its philosophy, and practice through a relational world view that embraces the observable and unobservable worlds of living and non-living elements.

In addition to that, the values of nature pedagogy run beneath all models of nature-based education and are manifested in many different educational models that exist around the world. No one model is supreme and perfect, but all models need to respond to location and cultural situation. All of these models are affected by a number of aspects.

One of those aspects is the view of the adults who work there. In some models, the natural world is viewed as 'the other' and the time spent with nature

Figure 3.1 Interconnected meshwork

is consequently reduced, the space it is given and the way it is treated are not framed for sustainability but for consumption. This chapter explores the tensions that exist between models of nature-based learning that have arisen from a narrow view of the relationships between the living and the non-living. It demonstrates that we need to be aware of becoming reductionist in our views of the natural world.

It would be useful to pause and consider your own view of what the natural world means to you as we delve into the many ways that we view it and indeed embed it in our practice.

CONSIDER

How would you describe your view on nature? Is it part of you or somewhere you visit?

In your experience, how do you think your colleagues view it?

Think of children. What moments can you think of where children seemed to have a real empathy with other living and non-living things?

Defining nature

In order to start the process of the definition of a pedagogy rooted in nature, let us think about what may be meant by using the word 'nature' itself. Nature is defined in two main ways in the Oxford English Dictionary (OED) (2018): '... the phenomena of the physical world collectively, including plants, animals, the landscape, and other features and products of the earth, as opposed to humans or human creations' and as 'the physical force regarded as causing and regulating the phenomena of the world'. This section examines the relevance of both definitions.

Physical world

... the phenomena of the physical world collectively, including plants, animals, the landscape, and other features and products of the earth, as opposed to humans or human creations. (OED, 2018)

This first definition positions humans outside of nature as it uses the word 'opposed to'. In this work, the word 'nature' is considered to be more encompassing and is defined through a relational lens as the living and non-living elements that are both observable and unobservable.

Figure 3.2   Birdsong

In the image in Figure 3.2 entitled 'Birdsong', there are several implicit messages. Does the image say birdsong to you? Are there other words that come to mind when you look at this image? Joy, vibrancy, energy, companionship, hunger?

Is it possible that in our drive to be dominant over the rest of the natural world, we have become so anthropocentric (human focused) that we give the other creatures in the natural world human-style emotions? Or is it a possibility that there are elements of the natural world that we cannot yet fathom?

Some people view humans as so superior to nature that they are no longer affected by it. This suggests that humans have evolved further through intelligence, as we see in the evolutionary work of Darwin, to be beyond the need or influence of things occurring out of sight in the natural world. Their dominion over nature, as Kellert (2012) calls it, gives them the sense that they can control and manage the natural world for human benefit. This group of humans view themselves as separated or detached and consequently view nature as *the other*. They are egocentric and often struggle to make a connection between their actions, such as pollution and waste management, and their own health as they are driven by the belief that nothing can affect them.

A second view is that humans are not removed from nature but are integral to it and so they live in a sustainable, balanced way along with the living and non-living. They are said to be ecocentric as the ecology of the Earth influences their values. These two broad and general views are shown visually in the images below, and although no-one can easily say they are eco- or egocentric, it is worthwhile to consider your own tendency as it will affect the decisions and choices you make.

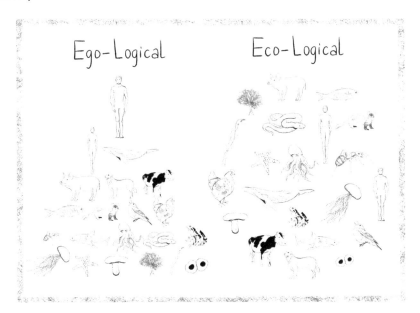

Figure 3.3 Egocentric and ecocentric (ego-logical and eco-logical) thinking. Influenced by Buss, 2005.

The language we use when we speak about nature belies our view of whether our intent is to learn *about* it, to be *in* nature or to be *with* nature, or to act *for* nature. Nature is perceived in a different way in each case (as discussed in Chapter 2), but all come together as discussed in a form of environmental kinship.

─────────────── **CASE STUDY** ───────────────

What is nature?

The children had been bringing into their play their knowledge of animals that live outside the climate of Scotland in the past and present. The dinosaur, rhino, tiger and elephant appeared regularly in the small worlds they create outside and the team had noticed the way that children dismiss certain animals as not as important. The predators were often chosen first and used in play that involved dominance and submission. Through looking at silhouettes of animals the conversation started with guessing the animals from all over the world and what they were called.

When the images were cut up, the children were asked to think whether there were any animals and plants that were more important. Humans were represented as a male and female outline; the children used them interchangeably using he or she, dad and mum in the conversation.

Figure 3.4   The ant makes the man jump

The images in Figure 3.4 show their first idea of creating a line related to the idea that importance is related to the size of the real animal until a child added the ant, saying 'it can make the man jump, so it's important'. This statement stimulated a change of direction about animals that bite and how that made them important and powerful.

Figure 3.5 'The man and the crocodile are important'

The debate about things that bite took us to the predators such as the crocodile, panther and tiger, so they were moved to the upper area of the group along with a baboon, just because they laughed every time they said the word. When asked about the male and the female, the children responded by saying, 'Yes, the man because he looks after all the others and drives the tractor', which is a connection to lived experiences outside the centre.

The children grouped many animals together, saying:

'This is the humans and the animals are all their friends.'

'It's everything all together.'

'Look, the butterfly has a friend.'

'There are the crocodile's friends.'

'Then the fish comes up and gets away fast from the crocodile.'

(Continued)

Figure 3.6 They are all together

It was at the end of the conversation when one of the children picked up the human outlines and took them away, saying 'They can all be friends, but not them. They have to go somewhere else'. This could have been part of the child's desire to carry on with a story about the humans or seen to be an action to separate and divide the humans from the rest of the natural world.

Figure 3.7 Humans removed from the natural world

Without an extensive research programme over months, it has limitations. However, the team found it interesting to reflect on children's perceptions of the relationships between the living elements of the natural world and how we portray the relationships in images, stories and resources. The images used did not include micro-organisms, plants or the non-living elements. There had been discussions about cycles and patterns of local animals like cows and sheep, but given the pandemic, the staff are wondering where they would place micro-organisms such as a virus.

From an adult perspective, there are two versions of nature that emerge from research. The first is the perception that nature is *out there* as something to visit and study and the second is that it is *culturally perceived*. The difference between the two and the definition of a third are key to this thinking and an understanding of what a fully embedded nature pedagogy seeks to be.

Nature out there

People who view nature as out there, as an 'observable, independent, external and scientifically verifiable reality' (Taylor, 2013: 67) or, as Ingold suggests, 'really natural nature' (2011: 41), are called 'nature realists' (Taylor, 2013: 67). The realists view nature as something to be scientifically studied and through this they validate objective facts that are shared with the public through theories and research papers, nature documentaries and school science curricula.

In the late 17th century, colonial practices on the part of the British clearly indicated that studying and collecting nature was the extent of their relationship with it. Even in modern Western society many people choose to be in nature, to walk over it and to take materials from it in a way that views it purely as a giant playground for the human race. One example of our changing relationship with nature is the growth in popularity of television series such as 'I'm a Celebrity, Get Me Out of Here' or other relatively extreme survival-type programmes where humans are pitted against nature and/or each other in structured feats or situations designed to test their ingenuity, resolve or resilience whilst the animals are already highly controlled.

One not dissimilar manifestation of this within education exists in nature-based programmes where poor site awareness and understanding of the balancing of needs of humans and land have resulted in extensive denudation of the site. What should have manifested itself as a desire to understand and be with nature appears in practice to become purely a survivalist type activity, which allows children to destroy the very landscape we need to consider.

The natural world and the children can both ultimately be disadvantaged in these cases, as the education programme and the benefits it was intended to deliver may never materialise in practice and the children concerned can be left with the impression that the behaviours learned in these environments are acceptable in all natural environments, with such behaviours completely failing to recognise the need for balance between the living and the non-living, between humans and the rest of the natural world.

Culturally perceived nature

The second version of nature is that rather than it being out there, nature is 'culturally constructed' (Ingold, 2011: 41). Taylor refers to some people in society as 'nature constructionists' (2013: 67). The nature constructionists do not engage with a singular view of nature, as the nature realists do, but suggest that nature is not only socially constructed but contingent upon the cultural, historical and political circumstances of its construction. Our understanding of nature pedagogy is that it changes through time, interrelated in many ways and unable to be detached from nature as we live our storied lives within our own time. Bronfenbrenner and Morris's social systems model (1998) could be seen to be very human centric as it does not integrate the more than human world, but shares the impact that we have on the natural world through the actions we take.

The need to not compare alternative views of the natural world but to look at two different ways of comprehending it was outlined by Ingold (2011). One is through the process of mental representation, whilst the other does not comprehend nature as a 'construction but of engagement; not of building but dwelling, not making a view *of* the world but of taking up a view *in* it' (Ingold, 1996: 117; emphasis added). The latter view aligns with relational world views that are central to nature pedagogy.

A force or phenomena?

The third definition is that nature is the physical force regarded as causing and regulating the phenomena of the world. There are two key phrases or words that resonate here. Firstly, that nature is seen to have a *physical force*, which is explored through the innovative work in quantum biology, in Chapter 4.

Secondly, it alludes to a more random experience through the word 'phenomena'. Phenomena is derived from the Greek *phainomenon* (that which appears or is seen). By considering the definition of 'appears' as something that is felt rather than seen, the possibility exists that nature is seen, and unseen, just as it is living and non-living. By adopting this definition, it is possible to examine nature pedagogy as being a way of working with children in an integrated way that embraces the unobservable phenomena of disruption and flux but also silence, peace and calmness experienced daily when outside under the open sky.

This pedagogy positions itself fully with the natural world, and as such, views a society of people connected to the environment in which they live through an unobservable and observable relationship. This reciprocal relationship is key to education as we begin to understand that the way we educate our children needs to change from reducing learning to component parts, separate and measured to be more sustainable – an education that acknowledges the rights of the planet and the organisms on it.

Inside, outside and beyond

In order to make this relationship across locations more accessible, we can reduce it to the three nominal spaces of inside, outside and beyond, as shared in the 'Mapping our place' case study in Chapter 2. Each of these locations has its own unique style as the spaces develop in very different ways according to sociocultural behaviours and the play affordance they offer.

We can explore the structure in these spaces as noted earlier through the use of space, time, adult role and resources (STAR). Some of these include the:

- space and how they organise it inside, outside and perhaps beyond
- time adults and children spend in them, and how they divide the time in a day
- perception of the adult role as stepping in or stepping back
- resources they choose to put into them or not.

The *inside* is under shelter or inside the building, the *outside* is the landscaped area around the setting and the *beyond* space was defined as 'a space beyond the gate, where nature is on nature's terms, not manicured, cleaned up or processed' (Warden, 2015: 29).

Lee-Hammond comments on the barrier that a gate metaphorically and physically presents in terms of legal requirements. She states, '... educators seeking support for outdoor play experiences in places beyond the school gate, what Warden (2015) describes as "beyond", it may be that those deciding on permissions are far removed from the realities of being in nature' (2017: 330).

Wilderness or a sense of wild

In the space beyond the gate, there is what could be called a more 'authentic space', although still affected by humans. Taylor argues for the deconstruction of the concept of wilderness in order to 'better understand its iron grip in contemporary Western, environmental discourses' (2011: 423). The world we refer to as natural has a long cultural history of Indigenous peoples who have shaped it and influenced its appearance through their harmonious, lived experiences. If we look at the work of Langton (1996), Plumwood (2003) and Spence (1999), they speak of un-peopled areas of wilderness that have in fact been historically populated by nomadic groups working with the natural world. The Western world seeks to conserve wilderness in a way that is rooted in the doctrine that the 'world of nature is separate from and subordinate to the world of humanity. Wilderness is therefore seen to be an environment that remains beyond the bounds of human civilisation as in a typical dictionary definition of a wilderness ... A tract of land or a region ... uncultivated or uninhabited by human beings' (Ingold, 2011: 67). This is problematic for many Indigenous peoples who reside in these areas, in that they are often included in the conservation ethic along with other flora and fauna, which reduces their status.

Figure 3.8 Wilderness?

The landscape of hills and mountains in Scotland is often portrayed as wilderness, but the hills are actually the scarred remains of massive deforestation and the introduction of non-native species brought about by human settlement that sought to master and use the natural world. Indigenous pedagogies do not take on a role that is dominant over the natural world, but are often subordinate to it, as we can read in the work of Nelson (1983), who writes about the Koyukon of Alaska:

> The proper role of humankind is to serve a dominant nature. The natural universe is nearly omnipotent, and only through acts of respect and propitiation is the well-being of humans ensured ... In the Koyukon world, human existence depends on a morally based relationship with the overarching powers of nature. Humanity acts at the behest of the environment. The Koyukon must move with the forces of their surroundings not attempting to control, master or fundamentally alter them. They do not confront nature; they yield to it. (Nelson, 1983: 240)

In this world view, there are not two worlds of humanity and nature, but one where the two intertwine, with humans actually being a small and somewhat insignificant part. In this doctrine, humans inhabit what Bird David (1992) refers to as a 'giving environment', where the natural world shares its food, shelter and resources.

Humans seek the concept of discovery of a pristine spot of wilderness and their quests take them further and further afield as access to very remote places opens up. Macfarlane (2017) suggests that they are seeking an emotive response as they no longer gain it from the simple wonderments that we used to feel towards a blade of grass. Let us question then, 'What is a wild space? Is it a place where we feel wild and free or a place where nature is free?' (Warden, 2010: 87).

We need to challenge the supremacy that humans feel they have over the natural world.

> In Western culture there has been such a move towards containing and controlling nature that you can go up mountains completely removed from the very elements you are going up there to feel. Do people travel in a car or train through a natural space to connect to nature or merely to conquer it and then say it has been claimed? (Warden, 2010: 87)

In the lived experience of Auchlone Nature Kindergarten, the spaces beyond the gate are what Heerwagen and Orians (2002) explore as wild natural spaces, disorderly, free ranging and untidy.

Perhaps we need to consider a sense of wildness (Warden, 2007), which is more akin to a sense of freedom physically, mentally and emotionally. This sense of wildness is shared in the nature pedagogy of Auchlone Nature Kindergarten as the space beyond the gate is actually in a process of constant flux, as it passes through time and therefore the lives of many living processes, each one leaving a small imprint on children's lives.

Nature and risk

Nature as *the other* is perceived and treated as a place that is riskful and is therefore given special treatment in terms of ratios and supervision, as evident in many outdoor play policies and forest school procedures. Any play outdoors is seen to push boundaries, test limits and involve risk (Little and Eager, 2010; Sandseter, 2009; Waller and Tovey, 2014), however our research (MacQuarrie et al., 2015) did demonstrate that there were cultural variations in the perceptions of nature as being full of risk.

In many cases, this subjectivity in the personal and cultural perceptions of the risk in nature pervades the decisions around ratios, areas, systems and educational procedures. An increase in anxiety over children's safety is currently the subject of extensive research (Gill, 2012; Lindon, 2011); however, this fear is sometimes linked to abduction *when outside* rather than the natural resources themselves, such as sticks and stones. The reality is that the figures related to abduction have not changed over the past 40 years or more (Lindon, 2011): what has changed is the adult response, by becoming an indoor dweller.

At different times in history and at different locations around the world there have been changes in our treatment of animals, from our need to defend ourselves from them to the need to defend them from us. We use the natural world to give us cheer through suggesting human traits such as smiling, as we can see in Figure 3.9 of the frog. The question of how we represent and treat animals in our day-to-day experiences with children is explored more fully in Chapters 5, 6 and 7.

Figure 3.9 We humanise animals

At this point, let us just acknowledge the power balance and the emotional vulnerability that is felt when working with children in the Australian bush compared to a forest in the UK. In Australia, one is subservient to nature in its power to inflict harm or death and the environment demands that you show some humility and respect. The power balance of being human in the face of an insect or reptile that can end your life awakens a sense of perspective that many of us have lost through their perception of human supremacy. Many people now live in spaces where any living threat has been removed or destroyed.

CONSIDER

- What are the experiences in your life that have affected your view of the natural world?
- How does your education and care practice reflect your own view of the natural world?

Reductionist views of nature

Knowledge at any given moment will be a function of our available means of perception of nature, for example through scientific investigation via a microscope.

In contrast to the reductionist views, Indigenous views of nature are holistic thinking and sit separately from some Western reductionist ideas. Reductionism separates nature into spiritual, moral, scientific and natural worlds, as evident in the work of Mere Roberts (Roberts and Wills, 1998; Roberts et al., 2004). In this reductionist model, there appears to be a 'them and us' division that permeates down to the education of young children. We see this in the environmental laws, operational licensing for education and curriculum design that restrict access to risk, keep different ages of children apart and create target-driven activities.

These aspects of policy and practice are affected by the holistic perceptions of people and place. Vine Deloria Jr. states that an Indigenous view of nature is a 'system in which all knowledge and experience is drawn together in order to establish the proper moral and ethical road or direction for human beings' (Deloria, 1999: 47). The Indigenous pedagogies therefore embrace the metaphysical world through their relational connections. Deloria and Wildcat suggest that in Native American culture:

> ... metaphysics was the realisation that the world, and all its possible experiences, constituted a social reality, a fabric of life in which everything had the possibility of intimate knowing relationships, because, ultimately, everything was related. (Deloria and Wildcat, 2001: 2)

This view of nature is mirrored in aboriginal writings. In this quote, Merindah writes a response to an *Australian Geographic* article about the discovery of DNA evidence relating to the connection of African people to Australian aboriginal people:

Have you heard of 'Tjukurrpa'? It is a word from my country, from the central desert tribes (I am Arrernte). In short: It is the Law which is handed down by right of birth to certain individuals within a tribe or nation which holds the knowledge of what links (the interconnectedness) the spiritual, human, physical and sacred worlds together and what they all mean in relation to one and other in all realms of existence.

It is the Law which governs our behaviour as humans with ALL other things in creation and the spiritual/sacred realm and each other. It also governs our responsibilities to all other things in creation and the spiritual/sacred realm and each other. It governs our kinship to all things. It explains everything else's relationship to the spiritual/sacred realm and to each other. (Merindah, 2017: 1)

Merindah's view of nature is not reduced to a scientific examination, rather she goes on to state the importance of 'the fundamental part of all life-spirit':

Science can argue it all they like, but science can only tell you what something is – the nuts and bolts of it all, but it cannot tell you why. It never tells you why. It can go down to the sub-atomic level and tell us that everything everywhere in the known universe is made up of exactly the same stuff – atoms, but it can't tell me why. It can try but it misses a fundamental part of all life – the spirit (for want of a better word). I honestly don't know how they can come up with any conclusions of any relevance if it refuses to take the spirit into account. There is more to life than what meets the eye. We have no beginning and no end, we are eternal. It's hard to grasp 'eternal' because we need to quantify things in our mind, and try and grasp the concept using 'time' and 'numbers'. You can't quantify it. No beginning means NO BEGINNING and no end means NO END. So you can't go back to the beginning, there isn't one. So I don't know why we keep looking. (Merindah, 2017: 1)

Moving on from exploring reductionist approaches, the next section explores the places of quantum science and metaphysics and the way that they challenge the status quo of some Western world views. Indeed, many findings explored in this chapter and the next support the view that nature is very much about observable and unobservable happenings.

Metaphysics and Indigenous knowledge

The relationship between Indigenous knowledge and metaphysics was visually presented by Johnson and Murton (2007) based on the work of Leroy

Little Bear (2000). The work by both explores holism and reductionism exemplified by two aspects of Newtonian science, which is associated with the laws of the observable, such as gravity, magnetism, inertia and so on, and quantum science, which can support us in understanding a quantum world where atoms and molecules do not behave according to our understanding of Newtonian science.

Newtonian science focuses on finite truths that can be explained through observable experiments. It developed narrow and singular truths and led the world into binary dualism. In this environment, the dualism led to the belief that learning and life were linear and that time was constant. What was believed to be true about the natural world through being observable is now challenged by the world of quantum science, especially the world of quantum biology, which is expanded on in Chapter 4.

This shifting world view has opened up the discussion around an interconnected, metaphysical space that may support an understanding of flux and patterns in the natural world. These patterns were felt and visually shared through art and story by First Nation, Indigenous peoples and should be publicly acknowledged and respected. The dominant Western world view held by some people is slowly moving from a basis of Newtonian science to embrace quantum theories where unseen aspects of spirit, flux, interrelated knowledge and process are acknowledged as valid within ways of knowing.

Arturo Escobar suggests that new styles of writing are evidence of a 'place-based consciousness, a place-specific (if not place-bound or place determined) way of endowing the world with meaning' (Escobar, 2000: 153). If this is so, it is possible that these new stories and accounts come with an opportunity, or as Johnson and Murton (2007) suggest, the ability, to influence and shape a new anti-colonial perspective.

Patterns and connections in the natural world

The natural world is full of patterns, an idea that is more fully developed in Chapter 4, and they are key to an understanding of quantum biology. Examples beyond the physical ones of whirlpools and wind patterns are created by many living things. In the examples in Figure 3.10, these Fibonacci spirals retain their shape as they grow, with no element remaining static. A spiral shell carries the snail's prochronism (a record of how, in its *own* past, it solved a problem of needing to grow through pattern formation). Patterns tend to be thought of as static, perhaps as a result of the snapshots recorded by media, but in reality they are dynamic.

Figure 3.10 Spirality in nature

To seek the pattern that connects us all in a related wholeness, Bateson suggests looking 'beyond the trivial (size, colour, race, sex, etc.) to a deeper, more hidden relationship' (1979: 8). When we look at the natural world, how often do we focus more on the aesthetics?

Stories are linked in First Nation thinking as shared in Leroy Little Bear's (2000) thinking in his work on the place of story. In storying, nouns are traditionally said to be words that define individual objects, rather than including and describing the relationship between the objects, so the words that need to be considered in relation to the natural world are verbs, such as caring, supporting and evolving.

CONSIDER

If you were to consult children, how do you think they would respond to the question 'What is nature'?

How does the awareness of the range of nature-based models affect your practice?

Tensions within nature-based models of education

Nature-based models of education are generally taken to be those that focus on either learning *about* nature, such as the nature-preschools in the USA that are rooted in their nature centres; or learning *in* nature, such as forest schools that take place in a wooded space; or learning *with* nature inside, outside and beyond, as seen in some nature kindergartens; or green schools that are creating the capacities and skills for the benefit of the rest of the natural world.

These models are all nature based, in that time is spent outside in the natural world, under the sky; but there are varying degrees of integration of the principles of nature pedagogy within them as they engage in elements of the pedagogy during visits, events or moments, but do not embrace the lived, interrelated experiences of nature pedagogy entirely.

The connection between nature pedagogy and forest school

The analogy used in Chapter 2 to describe the relationship between nature-based models and nature pedagogy is that of fungal mycelium representing an underlying adaptive pedagogy (Warden, 2015). This meshwork (Ingold, 2013) has many interconnections and branches. Unlike a network, where there are defined nuclei, the meshwork has an infinite number of patterns due to its state of flux and adaptation to the environment. In this analogy, the fruiting bodies are considered to be models of education. They are intentionally slightly different in response to place. All the nature-based settings are, however, connected through their values and the lived experiences that are influenced by nature pedagogy.

The level of engagement with nature pedagogy stretches from being segregated from the principles to a full integration with it. Nature pedagogy is unseen as a way of working until it is manifested in a model of practice. The fruiting bodies represent a range of models that sit above, but are still connected to, this mycelium. Unlike the rhizomatic thinking suggested by Deleuze and Guattari (2004) where the rhizome creates the same plant many times over, the models are all different due to the uniqueness of the physical and cultural environments from which they emerged (Gibson, 1979).

These models are known by names such as forest schools, outdoor nurseries, nature kindergartens, nature groups, nature-based outdoor play and *Skogsmulle*. Work that seeks to expand any one of these models, such as forest schools without adaptation to place, people and environment, is indicative of educational colonialisation.

A pedagogy of practice can spread globally, but the way it presents itself needs to be adapted to the cultural and physical location and it therefore creates situations that are relevant and respectful. Through doing this, it is possible to create a global meshwork of practice that is explored through the International Association of Nature Pedagogy (Chapter 7). If we take one model and place it in another geographical and cultural location, it effectively imposes a reductionist model on people's cultural and diverse physical environments. Further, I would argue that in some of the writing that supports forest schools, there are in fact not examples of one model, but there is a spectrum of models practising nature-based pedagogy.

Each model engages with the natural world in some way. For example, Knight's (2013) text has chapters on food production in South Africa (cited in Papatheodorou, 2013), Brazilian examples of sustainability (Grandisoli, 2013), a vehicle for play in Portugal (Figueiredo et al., 2013) and eco remediations in Slovenia (Krajnc and Korže, 2013) and includes a chapter entitled 'Play in nature: Bush kinder in Australia' (Elliot, 2013), which is more closely aligned to a forest school model in terms of frequency of occurrence but has a greater consideration of the rights of First Nation peoples. All these models have been grouped together by Knight (2013) as 'international forest school', which is problematic as they are not one model but evidence of pedagogical values.

In summary, nature is viewed as a place of pattern and connection, which we as humans share with living and non-living elements. Building on this definition of nature, there is a difference between nature pedagogy and models such as forest school. The former is a form of pedagogical thinking, which views nature through the Indigenous lens of a dynamic state described by a verb, in a place of constant flux and adaptation, which is felt through energy waves, central to spirit, interrelated, providing renewal for all its elements, and which is connected to process and space. Forest school is a model that has emerged from an observation by British lecturers, and although it has a set of principles, it is often still seen as a peripheral experience in schools.

The next chapter explores the phrase 'being with' and examines how important human connection to the rest of the natural world really is.

SUMMARY

- The natural world is a meshwork of interrelated elements; some of these elements are observable and some are not.
- Egocentric behaviours and approaches to decision making need to be changed to be more balanced and inclusive.
- Humans often remove themselves to see nature as 'the other', which leads them to wrongly assume that they will not be affected by issues such as climate change and loss of habitat.
- Patterns, connections and waves are present in all interactions with nature from a snail's shell to the galaxy. Humans are not always aware of them.

Four

Being with nature in a relational way

Chapter overview

Humans can learn *about*, be *in*, or learn *with* the natural world, and can act for the benefit of doing things *for* it. When embedded in everyday lived experiences, nature pedagogy is a way of being with nature, in an inclusive, sustainable, interrelated and spiritual way. For some people, being immersed in the natural world is a stimulus for religion and spirituality. However, rather than seeking the divine, as is the case in most world religions, it is a form of broad spirituality that seeks to support human sustainability. The field of quantum biology allows us to consider a relational world as shown in Chapter 3, not just macroscopic or thermodynamic relations, but those at invisible atomic, molecular and particle levels that do not obey Newtonian laws. It is these relations that are unobservable and yet affect all entities on the planet.

In order to comprehensively define 'nature pedagogy', this work must explore our place as humans in relation to the rest of the natural world. There are many types of relationships that could be explored, but for the purposes of this writing, four key aspects of relationships are selected that focus on *other*, *sustainability*, *spirit* and *nature as a whole*. In exploring the complexity and tensions around the sense of *being with* nature in these four ways, we can deepen our understanding of the relational world view that is central to nature pedagogy.

Connections to nature

The phrase 'connecting to nature' is used commonly in education to suggest some form of relationship that humans should develop with the natural world. It is possible, however, that humans have no choice but to be connected, as they are an integral part of the natural world.

A study by Giusti et al. (2018), which builds on the work of Heft (1988), suggests a framework for assessing the connectedness of children to nature. It cites ten qualities that can be used to evaluate a connective relationship: feeling attached to natural spaces; knowing about nature; reading nature spaces; acting in nature spaces; recalling memory; being curious; feeling comfortable in natural spaces; taking care of nature; caring about nature; and being one with nature.

This refers to *being one with nature* as linked to an ergo-centric view of our role to 'be for nature' (Giusti et al., 2018: 11) in terms of taking care of nature, rather than it ultimately being an integral part of our own human existence.

The research suggests that *being one with nature* is perceived by 67 per cent of international nature-based practitioners (from a diverse range and significant number of organisations) as being the *last* ability/facet of humans' natural connections to develop, whereas my research identifies it as fundamental and one of the *first* to develop in young children.

Research in the past 20 years has focused significantly on how people see themselves in relation to nature (Ives et al., 2017) and has tended to focus on two aspects. Firstly, that of landscape and urban design (Colding and Barthel, 2017; Lewicka, 2011): in its wider context, it has made the natural world accessible, but is the arrangement mutually beneficial? Secondly, that of deep-rooted connection(s) to the natural world in life, especially in childhood (Chawla, 1998, 1999; Evans et al., 2007; Hsu, 2009; Kahn, 2002) where the fascinations and immersion of the child in the natural elements result in complete absorption in the moment.

This book broadens these two aspects to explore the wider aspects of human connection to nature, such as the evolutionary explanations, of which Kellert and Wilson's (1993) work is an example. It also draws on Arne Naess's work

Figure 4.1   Benefit for humans or the natural world?

(1973) as we consider children's ecological identity and how children relate to nature to create a more ecocentric view of themselves.

The basic contention of the phrase 'relational' is that the relationships between entities are more fundamental than the entities themselves (Wildman, 2006). The use of the word 'relation' is challenging for a number of reasons. Firstly, there is such a potential variety and complexity of relationships to define (Wildman, 2006); the consideration of emotional, logical, mechanical, cultural, sexual, aesthetic, etc. contexts all provide such a range of what can be seen as possible types of relationship that it makes it impossible to characterise the term 'relation' in a single way.

An attempt to analyse simple relations and then to extend the analysis to complex ones is met with the challenge of who defines simple and complex? Who can truly create broad definitions when the picking of a flower could be seen as a simple relation of desire and function or as suggesting a deeper, more complex relationship to the whole of the natural world?

Secondly, when considering nature-based relations, they are omnipresent and can take many forms, such as dominionistic, spiritual, attraction-based, symbolic and exploitative (Kellert, 2012). The exploration of relationships that are more abstract moves into a philosophical way of thinking that is rooted in science, rather than traditional Cartesian philosophy. Within quantum science, biology and cognition within the brain–body relation, or indeed within quantum biology itself, there are too many possible relations to create a unified definition.

Thirdly, relations are personal and individual, some of which are linked to spirit, as explored in the work of Kellert (2012) and Tucker (2002), and often, but not in all cases, this seeks to connect to a single deity, as seen in the work of Schweitzer (1947).

The term 'relation' is therefore challenging to use. When we explore the stories that we experience each day when we work with children, we have a sense of *truth*, in that place, in that time, with those children.

The pedagogies of practice in many educational environments have been made to focus on the observable, so lists of tangible experiences have replaced the more complex and implicit world of relationships as shared in the diagram on knowledge systems in the previous chapter.

By way of contrast, there are various thinkers in contemporary Western education, including not only Friedrich Nietzsche and Martin Heidegger, but also Max Weber, Gilles Deleuze, Michel Foucault and others, who can be seen to influence the need for relational understandings.

Tensions of being *with* nature

In the introduction to this book, the phrase 'inside, outside and beyond' was identified as not only linked to spatial locations for play and learning, but as also representing a second, more complex metaphor linked to a relational world view. Nature pedagogy is also the art of being with nature inside, outside and beyond, in terms of the inside in relationship with the self, the outside in relationship with others and then the beyond, viewed as our relationship with the living and non-living worlds.

Every day we are in myriad relationships with the world around us. This chapter explores being with nature in some of those moments, simplified to four aspects:

- being with nature as the 'other'
- being with nature sustainably
- being with nature in spirit
- being with nature in an integrated way.

About, in, with and for

Ultimately, this chapter seeks to define what the phrase 'being with' nature represents within the definition of nature pedagogy. There is intent in the use of the word *with*, as opposed to being *on* or *in* or *for* nature, in that it suggests a different type of relationship. The semantics of the use of these small words changes the relationship: to learn about nature suggests it is something to be studied; to be in nature suggests that we can choose to move in or out of it at any point. Learning with it ensures that the natural world is the location, context and resource for playful learning. All these come together to create a sense of desire to act for the natural world, not because we are dominant but because we believe in the mutual benefits.

Figure 4.2 A sense of boundless enthusiasm

As described in the previous chapter, in the phrase 'nature pedagogy' the word 'nature' is all encompassing; a chaotic, constantly evolving, cyclical process of which our short, individual human existences are a part.

Being with nature as the 'other'

The first aspect to explore further is also a point that was explored in Chapter 3. The dominant discourse and behaviour appear to have changed to view nature as 'the other' rather than something that is part of our own sustainability as a human race.

We know more now than we have ever known about the natural world through books, social media and film; however, we also know, as shown earlier, that children are not spending as much time outside as they could be, either at home or in early childhood settings. This has affected our personal awareness and knowledge of the natural world.

There may be moments in our lives in which we do achieve a deep connect-edness, as an integral part of being outside in nature. Sobel suggests that to do so is a 'gift of middle childhood' (2008: 15). In support of this sensitive childhood period, anthropologist Cobb interviewed 300 European scholars and noted that there appeared to be:

> A special period, a little understood, pre-pubertal, halcyon, middle-age of childhood ... where the natural world is experienced in some highly evocative way, producing in the child a sense of some profound continuity and natural processes. (Cobb, 1959: 22)

Childhood is suggested as a time of open sensitivity for some Western children. However, Indigenous pedagogies note that this timeframe is not reduced to one stage but extended throughout life.

Figure 4.3 Developing empathy

In the United Nations World Charter for Nature (1982), it states in Section (a) that 'mankind is a part of nature and life depends on the uninterrupted func-tioning of natural systems which ensure the supply of energy and nutrients'. Although there is a suggestion here of relationship, it reveals its reasoning by stating that it is in relation to the sustainability of life for human benefit, rather than for the Earth and us as organisms on it. There is no mention of the place of nature in terms of emotional and spiritual health, which may be the cause of one of the most far-reaching impacts on humans' emotional wellbeing.

Being with nature sustainably

The second aspect is focused on sustainability, but the sustainability of the human race primarily is explored more fully in Chapter 6. We are aware that there is growing evidence of some children struggling to thrive, in that we have a growing obesity problem and growing issues with myopia, poor muscle tone and cardiovascular weakness.

The physical manifestations of these issues are readily observable, with mental illness and stress becoming increasingly evident. It is perhaps significant that these behaviours are becoming apparent at the same time as ready access to the natural world is being reduced. In the field of early education, the work of Richard Louv (2005) and his term 'nature deficit disorder' brought children's engagement with the natural world to wider public attention. Phrases such as 'reconnecting children to nature' are the tag lines used in many popular nature-based organisations. The issue for work in nature pedagogy is how to reconnect to something we are unable to separate from.

Mastery or humility

There are many models of nature-based education, as discussed in Chapter 3. All of the models that integrate nature pedagogy need to create a relationship with the natural world that ensures that children are safe and thriving. In order to do this, there need to be some physical adjustments made to the natural world to provide shelter, warmth and food. In some respects, we assert our dominion over nature for the care of children.

The term 'wooing of the earth' was inspired by Indian Indigenous poet Rabindranath Tagore and developed by Rene Dubos to suggest that humans should control and enhance nature for human benefit – an egocentric view of human dominion over nature that is underpinned by love. He states:

> The phrase 'wooing of the earth' suggests a relationship between humankind and Nature [can] be one of respect and love rather than domination ... the outcome of [this] wooing can be rich, satisfying and lastingly successful only if both partners are modified by their association so as to become better adapted to each other. (Dubos, 1980: 68)

Figure 4.4 Respect and love

If we treat the other parts of our natural world with respect, wisdom and restraint in how we use its resources, Dubos suggests that it will be neither biologically wrong nor culturally regrettable. However, the understanding of wisdom changes according to one's view of the world. In one example, Kellert suggests that 'a humble approach to mastering the land is far more likely to yield outcomes in which nature and humanity achieve a mutually productive and sustainable relationship' (Kellert, 2012: 88).

The challenge that faces us in our relationship with nature in a global context is that we have become removed from the effects of our actions and decisions to dominate it. In periods of history where people had a sense of *being with* the land, the effect of not gathering corn was felt in hunger, not noticing a broken fence would result in domestic animals escaping, or not collecting sufficient wool would result in a lack of cloth for clothing.

—————————————— CASE STUDY ——————————————

Frog friends

The outdoor landscape is real, observable and meaningful to children when they design and care for it. The area that children have access to over a week at the centre has many elements, as you will have seen from the map in Chapter 1. When the nursery came to this site, there was little diversity and a species audit showed little habitat diversification in the garden area. In order to consult children, the first Talking Tub was created with lines of inquiry around amphibians, birdlife, vegetables, flowering plants, visiting animals (such as Fidget the lamb). These main ideas (shown in the petals in Figure 4.5) had emerged from the children's plans around what they wanted on site and changed as their understanding increased and the site developed.

Figure 4.5   Talking Tub

Having decided to explore amphibians, one child chose frogs and created a visual mind map of what he knew but also included the images from the Talking Tub that connected to him, which was noted by the adult at the end of the session.

The ongoing cycle of planning, care and maintenance can be long term, so site Floorbooks® are kept for years to monitor impact, both good and bad. In 2016, the children created the pond; five years later, in 2021, it was time to redo the pond liner and change the design to accommodate the increased diversity in the garden, which included toads, common frogs and newts. The cycle of maintenance and care ensures that the site is pesticide and chemical free, but it has to be an integral part of the daily routines with children, or it becomes unmanageable.

The new designs for the site included:

'rocks, islands, walking ramps'

'little paths so we can waltz around'

'spaces for them to croak'

'ponds for them to move around in'.

(Continued)

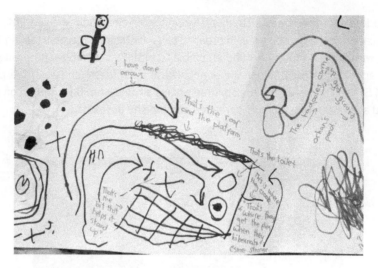

Figure 4.6   Spaces for them to croak

The understanding to contribute to the habitat has helped in the understanding of the role of the animals, for example Pipistrelle bats help us to control midges and insects that bite us in the summer months if we protect their nursery roost in the roof of the cottage. Physical action to protect does suggest that humans are dominant over the rest of the natural world as we seek to save it, but the children talk about the other animals on site as friends. So perhaps it becomes an adult perception to be dominant over the natural world rather than a child's.

When decisions are made that are removed from location and cultural contexts, as we now see increasingly in a growing reliance on global markets, we risk a whole range of both apparent and unseen consequences. Through experiences, as shared above, children come to value the flora and fauna of their local environment. The dominant discourse of modern, large-scale development 'typically encourages profound environmental and social perturbations, the production of enormous wastes and pollutants, and a growing separation of people from nature' (Kellert et al., 2008: 23). We can see this in the desire for high carbon footprint to import exotic, non-native resources from all over the world to help children in settings feel more connected. Ironic, isn't it?

Being with nature in spirit

The third aspect is incredibly complex and cannot be fully examined as part of a single book, but it does warrant mention, as the majority of writing on nature-based education does not address it. Kellert (2012) suggests that people's lives are enriched by their sense of existence and its connection to something of worth and value. It is this faith in the meaning of life that brings people together into a community of common beliefs. Religion, however, is described as 'the organized expression of spiritual belief, revealed in formally articulated principles and practices shared by a group of people' (Kellert, 2012: 100). Through consideration of this definition there are some apparent similarities with the principles and practices emerging in nature pedagogy but it is not defined as a religion.

This section explores this point further to examine whether there is an aspect of spiritual relationship that could be described as *being with* nature and to touch upon some examples of how it may be represented.

Holmes Rolston remarked, 'nature is a philosophical resource, as well as a scientific, recreational, aesthetic or economic one. We are programmed to ask *why?* And the natural dialectic is the cradle of our spirituality' (1986: 88). In this programmed state, the questions abound and the key one for this section is – what meaning does the word 'spirit' have in my work in relation to being with nature?

I personally don't need a *visit to nature* to have a sense of connection. I do, however, feel more at *ease* whenever I do. This wholeness and a way of 'being with' pervades everything in everyday life. However, much of the writing around mysticism and Western views of spirituality link either to a key moment in childhood or to a location in a natural landscape, which are typically recalled as shifts in feeling.

When we have a feeling that we describe as spiritual or religious, it is a 'mystical outcrying' (Steinbeck, 1941: 93) that appears to be prized and revered by people. What if this response, this spiritual feeling, is a recognition and an attempt to say that 'man is related to the whole thing, related inextricably to all reality' (Steinbeck, 1941: 94)? It may be that this profound emotion:

> . . .made a Jesus, a St. Augustine, a Roger Bacon, a Charles Darwin, an Einstein. Each of them in his own tempo and with his own voice discovered and affirmed that all things are one thing and that one thing is all things – a plankton, a shimmering phosphorescence on the sea and the spinning plants and an expanding universe. (Steinbeck, 1941: 94)

This would suggest that humans have been experiencing moments of *being with* nature throughout history, but did not have the collective language or the global awareness to make the connections.

Mysticism, spirit and ethics

The concept of nature mysticism was explored by Robinson (1977: 159) when he posed the question, 'Was there a sense that their lives had in any way been affected by some power beyond themselves?'. The results indicated that 15 per cent of a sample of 4,000 people responded that they had, and a significant proportion of those were related to experiences in nature. This could be taken to suggest a deeper connection to a mystic aspect of the natural world, a spiritual dimension that suggests the presence of 'other', albeit not in a human form.

Some writers view relationships as being more embracing of all aspects of the natural world, rather than just human-to-human, and in this way, they align themselves more closely with Indigenous philosophies. Inclusion of inanimate objects within land ethics touches upon the sense of community that Leopold (1949) explores. He suggests that we should link ethics with the human sense of community:

> All ethics so far evolved rest upon a single premise: that the individual is a member of a community of interdependent parts. His instincts prompt him to compete for his place in the community, but his ethics prompt him also to cooperate. The land ethic simply enlarges the boundaries of the community to include soils, waters, plants and animals, or collectively; the land. (Leopold, 1949: 30)

A biotic community defines a community as having an unseen force. He suggests that it is 'not merely the soil; it is a foundation of energy flowing through a circuit of soils, plants and animals. Food chains are the living channels which conduct energy upward; death and decay return it to the soil' (Leopold, 1949: 239).

The human is shaped by the biotic ethics that surround all the elements within the community and in turn those living and non-living aspects of the natural world have rights that can be protected, just as humans have rights. In 2016, 67 years after Leopold was published, New Zealand was the first country to use the World Charter for Nature to give equal rights to a piece of land and to humans (Te Urewara Act, 2014).

Reduction of relations

This will-to-power process is observed in many ways. Some humans reduce the importance of the natural world in their lives, but also reduce the status and rights of the peoples who live with it. We inadvertently affect ourselves as we reduce our perception to the fundamental thinking of the 'I', which in turn excludes the need for relationship or indeed community.

The effect of the reduced relationship between the head and the heart is further detailed by Rockefeller and Elder (1992) through a list of divisions that have occurred as a result of this reductionist action. Relationships have become divided 'between science and faith, fact and value, spirit and nature, ultimate meaning and everyday life, the sacred and the secular, the individual and the community, the self and god, male and female, and oppressor and oppressed' (Rockefeller and Elder, 1992: 154). In this list, they suggest a separation between spirit and nature, which resonates with the work of Leroy Little Bear (2000).

Some people move to religion to find relationships in both the physical and spiritual paradigms. Mary Evelyn Tucker (2002) identified four paths that world religions have taken to connect the experience of nature to spiritual revelation and understanding:

- Nature as a metaphor, offering a path or stepping stone to the divine.
- Nature as a mirror, a reflection and expression of the divine.
- Nature as a matrix, the place where people experience the divine.
- Nature as material, the means of being in touch with the divine.

In this book, I argue that society needs to embrace nature pedagogy in order to create a new, more educational pathway, which is not focused on seeking the divine, but one that supports human sustainability. Its focus would be nature in an integrated relationship, connecting the living and the non-living as elements of earth, fire, wind and water that help us to uncover the connections and patterns all around us.

In supporting practitioners to consider this aspect of their practice, it is hoped that they will embrace the fact that relationships with the natural world develop, irrespective of time, space and resources (Warden, 2015), and are not dependent on being in rural spaces but anywhere on the planet.

Developing a more ecological world view with which 'spiritual insights into nature and a rich vocabulary of imagery, symbol and metaphor' (Rockefeller and Elder, 1992: 158) would enable us in the West to develop and maintain a closer relationship with the natural world as a whole. Many more modern religions, such as Dark Green Religion (Taylor, 2009) and proponents of nature-based early learning, are inspired by the words of John Muir:

> Wonderful how completely everything in wild nature fits into us, as if truly part and parent of us. The sun shines not on us but in us. The rivers flow not past, but through us, thrilling, tingling, vibrating every fibre and cell of the substance of our bodies, making them glide and sing. The trees wave and the flowers bloom in our bodies as well as our souls, and every bird, wind song, and tremendous storm song ... is our song. (Muir, 1988: 5)

In contrast to spirit being in the living and the non-living, Muir was seeking connection with a single deity, which he referred to as God. He writes that, 'no dead, dry, box buildings, however grandly spired and coloured will ever bring us to true and healthy relations with the creator as will these bold wilderness groves' (Muir, 1988: 4).

Nonetheless, he writes of living in 'right relation' to nature in order to achieve lives of purpose and fulfilment. This is explored in the contemporary nature-worship called Deep Green Religion, where proponents seek to explore what might be called 'right relations'. They do this through living in a way that views nature as sacred, intrinsically valuable and requiring reverence and care. Although this does link a moral and ecological standpoint with an integrated system, it seeks enlightenment and is therefore focused on a spiritual gain. There is evidence that something occurs when we are *being with nature*, but the extent to which I can refer to it as 'spirit', as defined by the religions above, is limited.

CONSIDER

Our own views affect what we do in practice with children. What are the areas of your relationship with the natural world that could be developed to provide a deeper understanding?

Being with nature in an integrated way

When using continuums, we can consider the way that the many and varied models of nature-based education around the world develop their systems of working. Within those models, the use of time, space, resources and the adult

Table 4.1 Continuum of practice

	Segregated	Visiting	Integrated
Space	Defined and created by adults	Adult-created, nature-based landscape	Landscape invites settling and shelter
Time	Scheduled short blocks up to an hour	Daily blocks of time	Flexible according to energy levels. Access all day, every day
Adult role	Structure learning activities	Invitations set up for children	Co-constructed learning
Resources	Areas and commercial resources provided	Resources taken out with some loose parts	Resources are discovered and open ended

Adapted from Warden, 2015.

role were identified (Warden, 2015) as the four aspects required to organise and achieve learning. A consideration of each aspect and how it is used can be developed to chart a continuum of practice that moves from minimal planned contact with the natural world through to complete immersion in it for 100 per cent of the time that children are in the setting.

At one end of the continuum, the educational model is segregated from nature pedagogy, in that there is little evidence of the philosophy in practice, which Buber (1923) refers to as an 'I–It' relationship and which Foucault describes as 'self-interest':

> Everywhere nature is ordered and reordered, mobilized, and reworked to suit the ends dictated by human beings and most especially in relation to rationalized notions of our 'self-interest'; it is continually reduced to exchange-value within a modern market society; the earth is torn asunder at great ecological cost for the sake of extracting the 'resources' buried within. Phenomena are carefully and continually studied so that we may know them; but always at work in this is the fundamental drive to increase the extent of our control over the physical world. (Foucault, 2005: 14)

In order to give a general example, at the segregated end of the continuum, the natural world is viewed and treated as the other, with minimal contact and a high focus on control and educational curricula that reduce learning to outcomes and experiences. Time is therefore timetabled, space tends to be over-structured and resources supplied. The adult does not need to enter a relationship with either the child or the land in order to complete their work, as they can use directive, human-made materials and spaces.

The central area of the continuum has been referred to as 'visiting the natural world', as a reflection of the practice of taking indoor materials and resources into the natural world, rather than exploring the materials that nature provides. The adult relationship here becomes one of accountability to a set of learning objectives in a curriculum, whether set out at the start or at the end of the experience.

The right-hand end of this continuum, termed 'Integrated' with the natural world, illustrates the relationship with both child and land, in that the pedagogy of practice views ourselves as integral to the natural world. The relationship is therefore a meshwork (Ingold, 2011: 70) of many things intertwining, rather than the human as separate and objective to the natural world, where they view nature as the other.

In Chapter 7, the implications for practice give us practical guidance of things to consider that move us in our understanding of being with nature.

Relational world view

Relational views appear in many fields, such as theology, philosophy, psychology and educational theory. Here we use it to denote a relation in *being with the natural world*. Nature pedagogy does not separate mind, body and soul but rather supports a relational approach (Altman and Rogoff, 1987). The work of Gibson (1979) on affordance theory is significant here as it frames a relational approach to human perception and behaviour that is defined by the relations that exist between humans' abilities and the features in an environment (Chemero, 2009). As with many facets in education and as noted in the previous section, Gibson's (1979) work is often reduced to focus on physical loose materials, rather than the social or cultural aspects of his theory. While different understandings exist, affordances are defined as 'relations between abilities to perceive and act and features of the environment' (Chemero, 2009: 150).

Kyttä states, 'Gibson hardly wanted to divide the world up into material, social or cultural worlds, as he was against all division of environmental experience' (2003: 76). It is significant that now education has focused on the easier placement of loose parts in settings, there has been a development of the emotional affordances detailed by Roe and Aspinall (2011) and the social affordances explored by Kyttä (2006) in an assessment model of human–environment relations. Creating an embodied ecosystem (Raymond et al. 2017) is one of the most recent formulations of Gibson's theory. Raymond et al. (2017) contend that a set of relations emerges from between mind, body, culture and environment, within the context of environmental planning and management in an approach they refer to as 'embodied ecosystems'.

Figure 4.7   Green infrastructure

The work on embodied ecosystems draws on the three key assumptions that they are relational, situational and dynamic. Through using these three assumptions, the suggestion is that perception and action are the relations that are superimposed onto mind activity, body activity, the culture and the environment.

Humans do have a variety of relationships with the elements of earth, fire, air and water every day and yet they are challenging to define from our day-to-day perspective. We can use different ways of looking at these moments, and the final aspect of this chapter takes a leap down into the field of quantum science to consider that the relation is personal, subjective and in a constant state of flux, as suggested by Leroy Little Bear (2000).

CONSIDER

- How does the idea of the hidden quantum world affect how you view the world around you?

The lens of quantum biology

This section explores being in a whole relation with the natural world through the invisible world of quantum biology, in order to argue that human relations are affected by sub-atomic forces, in common with the living and the non-living

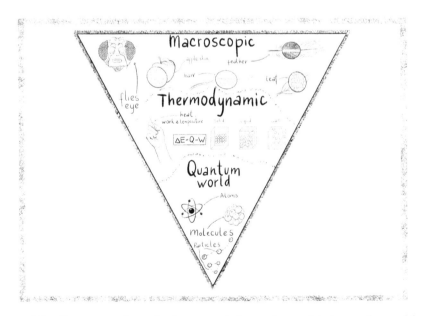

Figure 4.8   Representation of a framework from observable to unobservable elements

natural worlds. The macroscopic area has visible natural entities that adhere to Newtonian mechanical laws, thermodynamics has partially visible effects that adhere to some Newtonian laws, and the quantum world does not obey Newtonian laws and is largely invisible.

This relational view of the natural world as one entity has been explored by philosophy, religion and Newtonian science. However, Figure 4.8 shows the developing understanding that links observable natural entities to unobservable, subatomic particles, which can only be identified through their tangible or visible effects as they are too small to be seen by any normal means.

The field of quantum science is 'a mathematical framework that is absolutely logical and consistent and accurately describes the way the world is at the level of fundamental particles and forces' (Al-Khalili and McFadden, 2014: 290). Although it is logical, consistent and accurate, it rarely influences educational research as it sits in its own sphere of research. It is a challenge to our educational philosophies around nature-based learning, as to date we have relied on observable behaviours to explain what children are doing and feeling.

Quantum science has come to theorise the natural world through the field of quantum biology. In this relatively young field, researchers are able to consider the behaviour of the natural world through its smallest entities – molecules, atoms and even smaller than that, protons and exciton – the very smallest 'particles'. However, quantum biology is challenging to research or indeed explain in an education-focused book, as it pushes the boundaries of what we think of as scientific truths. It is included here to challenge what we believe to be true about the dualism of living and non-living entities and to introduce the possibility of unseen worlds that affect humans at a cellular level.

Quantum biology is a field of work that is ordinarily invisible to us. It is only when we observe the behaviour and patterns of individual molecules, such as the double-slit experiment in modern physics that some readers may recall from school, that we start to become aware of some of the fundamental quantum laws. Multi-modal learning, especially the use of film, has allowed scientists to create films that make this invisible life accessible.

There are several rifts in thinking (Caputo, 1987) that become apparent when we develop an understanding of the natural world through quantum biology. In fact, this field challenges the knowledge of the existence of life itself beyond Newtonian and Darwinian understanding, which for many, feels like a step too far. Children have no such barriers and are open to the idea of bird decision making and how they migrate because 'they just know in their hearts how to come back to their friends', and that birds' nests are brown 'because they don't have a choice'.

One key aspect to note is that of 'quantum tunnelling', which allows protons to *leak* through what appear to be solid structures. The protons move through every living object through enzymatic reactions, and although this is not referenced explicitly to the non-living, it does demonstrate that matter is not as solid as it may appear. Solids are in fact permeable to protons and, as Ingold (2011) suggested, on a journey with us, not static in time.

Al-Khalili (2014) goes further in his film documentaries to look into the behaviour of excitons that searches out a reaction centre within a plant cell in order to photosynthesise. Newtonian physics cannot explain how the exciton finds the reaction centre as it has no means of detecting it. Studies now suggest that the exciton behaves like a quantum wave and 'moves out on all routes simultaneously ... it's following all paths at the same time' (43:42). This work suggests that particles with 'definite positions could be taken seriously but also invoke the idea of a wave-like entity that links objects behind the scenes in ways that ordinary experience does not register' (Wildman, 2006: 8).

As we struggle to find some connected understanding of being with nature and perhaps life itself, the messages and possible explanations offered by quantum biology resonate with Leroy Little Bear's (2000) inclusion of 'energy waves' within Indigenous pedagogies detailed in Chapter 2. It also opens up the possibility of multiple ways of knowing to all humans, as Al-Khalili (2014) states in the film 'perhaps the ultra-modern world of quantum mechanics is actually an ancient fact of life' (46:50).

The second key point to take from this scientific work is the statement in relation to Western society's reductionist tendency to separate and disconnect, rather than include and integrate, as we see in Indigenous, holistic philosophies. With reference to the Newtonian, reductionist tendencies of science to subdivide and study, one of the researchers commented that 'we all had to come together to understand the relevance of this, we couldn't do it alone' (45:15). The separation of science and art is one dualism, but this extends within science itself into the fields of biology, physics, chemistry and so on. The scientist in this research field supports the integration and relationship of many aspects within a meshwork, to gain some clarity around *being with* the natural world. The sense of unique relation may be our awareness of the natural world, but ultimately it needs us to talk as educators and teachers with other professionals outside education, to debate and to create holistic understanding if we are to have any lasting impact on the sustainability of the natural world.

If we can accept that we are biased at the very root of our cultural attitudes to the non-human world, then we can begin to move forward to consider what the non-human world has to contribute to our understanding of the sustainability of humans and therefore create educational programmes that allow children to flourish.

A challenge to this relational world view is the presence of selfish, human tendencies that seek to continue to the benefit of certain groups of people at the expense of the other. At the very least, we must ask questions about human relationship with the rest of the natural world and be open to the possibilities of change for the benefit of the Earth and ourselves. The following chapters explore what we can do in our practice to make a difference.

——————————————— **SUMMARY** ———————————————

- Humans can learn about, be in, think with or act for the natural world. That is their choice to make.
- Nature pedagogy is a way of being that is sustainable, inclusive, interrelated and often spiritual.
- Humans try to reduce their relationship with the natural world as they seek to control it.
- The world of Newtonian science and mechanical laws are ways of thinking about the world, but they have limitations. Quantum thinking opens up human awareness of the possibilities of the unobservable world.

Five

Values and principles in practice

Chapter overview

This book has explored the theory behind nature-based pedagogies and now moves into the practical examples and applications of this work. This chapter explores what this thinking looks like in a set of adult behaviours, values and principles for practice. When we embrace these, we can make a difference in the transformation of early years practice from ergocentric to ecocentric.

Nature-based practice is the operation and application of a pedagogy, and the name suggests that it takes place in the natural world and does not necessarily involve a world view centred on relationships, but rather that nature is the provider of materials and a space to be used in learning. Nature pedagogy is a relational way of learning, teaching and development that embraces the living and the non-living world as a way of being with the observable and unobservable aspects of the world around us.

But so what? In terms of the history of this planet, human lifetimes are largely insignificant in their individual impact. What impact can there be of one person's thinking? Perhaps part of the answer lies within the use of research to challenge and provoke new perspectives.

Exploring values and principles

Although there are many benefits to working with pedagogical values that place the unobservable and the observable natural world at the centre of practice, there are also limitations.

The level of professional language in daily discourse between adults does not always afford the level of detail and complexity required to really debate the place of an unseen world or spirituality in their own and young children's daily lives. This theoretical content is not readily accessible, and although there is a growing interest in the spiritual relationship between the unobservable and observable worlds in early education, it is an under-researched field. As noted later in Chapter 7, the reflection needs to be embedded before, during and after encounters with children, so that practitioners can apply and consider concepts, over long periods of time in a secure, professional forum.

Keeping up to date with current thinking is a challenge for any early year's environment, and even when the research is made available, the integration of the values may only really become understood and embedded in practice after many years. The values identified in practice here were based on the narrative that practitioners shared through the graphics and film-making process over several years. They were collectively selected and endorsed by the team as those that felt right at that time in that space.

The principles that arise from these values influence the actions of the practitioners and therefore are foundational in defining a place-based nature pedagogy. The culture, climate, curriculum and community create a pedagogy of place that provides unique outdoor environments.

In some cases, pedagogical reflexivity (the thinking about the balance of power) is affected by the methods defined by an approach. Practices are

Figure 5.1 Culture, climate, curriculum and community influence a sense of place

influenced by theorists such as Montessori, Froebel and Steiner; others align themselves with a model such as forest school or *Skogsmulle*; and some with the defined practice in centres in a specific location, such as Reggio Emilia. Each theorist, model or location creates an identity around itself.

The practice in different places needs to be developed according to the location, but further than that they can all be more inclusive by sharing values that we align ourselves with, as they place the natural world at the centre of the choices and decisions they make. It is these values that connect nature-based practices across the globe, in a meshwork like the mycorrhizal network discussed earlier, which connects individual plants together to transfer water, nitrogen, carbon and other minerals. In the case of education, we could share ideas, research, innovation and support, rather than divide and separate to achieve an unbeneficial hierarchy of practice. Our communication as practitioners would be more inclusive if we connected through values that work with the natural world.

Values

In a pedagogical sense, values are fundamental qualities that guide or motivate attitudes/actions referred to as our behaviours. They help us to determine what is important to us. Values are essential to ethics as they are concerned with human actions and the choice of those actions. Ethics evaluates those actions and the values that underlie them. It determines which values should be pursued and which should not. Nazam and Husain (2016) suggest five broad types of values that were evident in school-aged children in India. In their work to explore spiritual values, they suggest that it is the integration of the values of the human soul consisting of altruistic, humanistic, personal and collective values that lead to spiritual growth of personality.

- Altruistic values refer to values promoting spiritual growth of personality, such as truthfulness, kindness, repentance, modesty, unity, charity and love.
- Humanistic values refer to values guiding our system that we use when we get accustomed to behaving with others. These values are more useful for promoting humanity, such as sincerity, justice, goodness, forgiveness, courage, power and wisdom.
- Personal values are those values that guide an individual to be perfect and get reinforced in personal relationships, such as self-restrain, selflessness, steadfastness, humility, righteousness, forbearance and fortitude.
- Collective values help to develop peace within the self and live in harmony with others, such as tenderness, gentleness, and contentment. (Nazam and Husain, 2016: 32)

Although some of these qualities such as forgiveness, wisdom and contentment may not be seen as values, the message is clear. Given that this book explores the relationship between humans and the rest of the natural world, let us extend this to include ecocentric values.

- Ecocentric values are those values that place the natural world (ecosphere) at the centre rather than human beings at the centre of decision making (anthropocentric). This ecocentric thinking moves beyond just the Earth's organisms (biosphere) as being of central importance, as it includes the living *and* the non-living elements.

Humility, openness, empathy and respect are some of the ecocentric behaviours and values that could influence and guide corporate and governmental policy makers when they make decisions that focus on a balance with the ecosphere.

When our ethics place the natural world at the centre of decision making, our values are being lived every day through the small things we do. When we focus on the values that underpin our philosophies, we can see how they in turn emerge into how we work with children, in essence the principles of our pedagogy.

CONSIDER

How do you support your colleagues to explore their ecocentric thinking through principles of practice?

Does your method of training align with the setting's core values?

Principles

Principles are based on a person's values, and in the case of larger organisations, the values of the leadership group. Principles inform or influence choices and actions across a wide range of roles and contexts. Successful evolution in culture, systems and practices across diverse agencies that connect in some way to the child may depend partly upon a shared philosophy and value base. When one group of practitioners embraces nature-centric ways of working and a visiting support worker or another colleague does not, a tension can emerge in how to move forward to create consistent practice.

————————————— CASE STUDY —————————————

Finding meaning in our practice

The words we use provide an insight into the values that guide practice, and in this example, drawings, words and imagery were all used to share thinking within a team. Research and policy creation have traditionally sat apart from the day-to-day experiences of practice to be something created by the leadership team, but with the emergence of practitioner research and the understanding of the power of participatory leadership, the stories that we spoke of in Chapter 2 start to emerge. It was decided by the team at Auchlone Nature Kindergarten to engage in self-evaluation and learning as adults in five different ways:

- Being aware of reciprocity and connectivity to being outside.
- Exploring material properties of local items, such as wool and grass.
- Being aware of emotional connection as an adult.
- Engagement in practical knowledge of the natural world.
- Changing and adapting materials to create an artefact (woven plaid) to stimulate dialogue.

Figure 5.2   The plaid

Given the belief that children learn when they have agency and are hands on, the staff team decided to explore their own learning in the same way. They decided to create a woven artefact made from wools collected and dyed with plants nearby, grasses made into cordage to hold artefacts, such as feathers and sticks found in their place. The plaid (Scottish long cloth) was made on a traditional ankle loom over several weeks. During this process, the team talked about their values. These cloth words were threaded through the plaid.

The words that resonated with the team were the words *spirit, nurture, growth, respect, pride, love* and *family.* This process of art-based experience allows practitioners to spend time together beyond operational conversations into the process of defining the values that motivate them in their practice, just as children's physical engagement with materials supports thinking and aids retention.

This plaid or long cloth was linked to place and the process of making it was recorded in words and film.

Further to the words noted above, the ongoing process of doing, making and thinking, framed by Martin (2003) as Indigenous research, gives us the space and time to note down broader principles of practice and how they may appear in practice. The principles connect us in our international focus on nature pedagogy and are key to avoiding educational reductionism and colonisation.

Positional

The natural world is placed at the centre of the programming as nature pedagogy asserts that children learn with, in, about and for the natural world. This is different from only being in nature as a location or learning about nature as a subject. When principles are integrated into practice, nature pedagogy offers both site and situations simultaneously. The resource is the natural world inside, outside and beyond; the time is in tune with nature's rhythms and flow; the adult is knowledgeable and skilled about the natural world in the place they work.

Positioning the pedagogy ensures that we respond to climate, culture, curriculum and community, as shared in Figure 5.1. This means that we embrace the situatedness of what we do. It includes natural rhythms of the climate, daily weather, seasonal produce and the resources they provide. Children are taught how to recognise their own circadian rhythms of energy, hunger and sleep. In the example of Auchlone, they are provided with options for pacing themselves, making, eating food and resting in the 'nest' or sleeping in the cabin or in hammocks in the forest.

Balanced

The power balance in relationships between adult and child influences the hidden or null curriculum, and benefits from being overt to young children so they are clear about what is happening, their role and what they are being expected to do (if anything).

In many of the nature-based models, *nature* is held up and presented as valued in different ways. In this nature pedagogy, the outdoor environment is the location, context and resource, all of which require us to be mindful of our relationship with it.

The graphic in Figure 5.3 gives an overview of the growth of thinking from the words that had meaning to the team, as shown in the case study, to the development of values explored earlier, and finally to define the principles. This chapter moves now to explore each principle in turn and share ways that they may be seen in practice.

Relational – friends, family, community, animals, plants and land

Relationships between the living and the non-living, and the observable and non-observable, are the focus of the everyday practices in the setting. This nature pedagogy focuses on the inside self, outside in relation with others and beyond in how we operate as a society.

Priority is given to the development of emotional resilience and a sense of self develops through allowing children to engage in the intellectual, physical and emotional challenges that the natural world offers them all day long, all week.

- Children have many moments of silence to be with the natural world, swinging on a branch, sitting by the base of a tree. These quiet moments are full of thinking rather than moments of emptiness. These moments of unobservable connection take place and offer a calm sense of being.
- The heart of the pedagogy is the relationship between the living and the non-living aspects of the natural world and it is seen as we care for plants, or have areas where we cannot go.
- The local community join us through everyday ritual and routines such as buying vegetables from the mobile library and shop.
- The children at Auchlone are aged from two years old to six years old, and as such, work like a family.

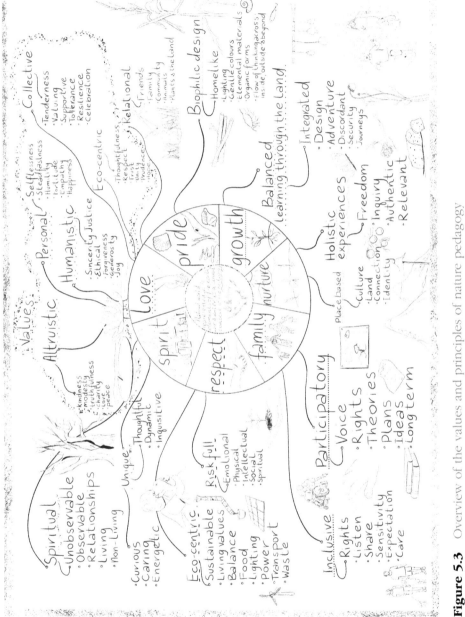

Figure 5.3 Overview of the values and principles of nature pedagogy

- The patience, joy and frustration are often visible in the play, but this is seen to be a key part of the social development of children.
- The skill of walking alongside rather than leading children is developed in the team.

Biophilic by design – homelike, lighting, colour, materials, forms, flow

The whole ethos of the three spaces of inside, outside and beyond demonstrates a love of the natural world. Kellert's (2012) work builds on ancient wisdom of the place of the four elements in what we now refer to as 'biophilic design'. They are embedded inside through the environmental features of natural décor (colour and materials); the elements of water, air, fire (sunlight) and earth; and landscape, both urban and rural. However, rather than residing in a single location, it bridges three: inside the built environment; the creation of native ecosystems outside in landscaped areas; and beyond into the wilder spaces where nature is *discovered*.

CASE STUDY

Rhythms of experience

The challenge in supporting people to understand the values that drive your thinking is that they are unobservable unless they affect daily practice. The small actions you take every day, the tone of your voice, the way you position yourself to talk with children are subtle but impactful.

Conversations around rhythms and rituals that have evolved over many years have led the value of holistic to be represented as the emotional aspect of seasonal change and how this in turn affects the opportunities that children encounter. These experiences sit in the domain of craft or folk pedagogy as they involve the ancient skills of harvesting, handling and use of the tangible materials, but they also reside in concept-based thinking that is expansive and not necessarily tangible.

Everywhere in the world has rhythms and transitions, from day to night, from wet to dry, from movement to stillness. In Scotland, there is a flow between four broad seasons but actually the transitions are much more subtle. Each day has many types of weather, and animals and plants do not appear on the timeframe of humans. Each day brings an unexpected new element that can offer a provocation or invitation for children to engage. Figure 5.4 offers an example of how the principles work in relation to creating a concept-led curriculum that works with rather than against the annual rhythms between humans and the four elements of earth, fire, air and water that they encounter.

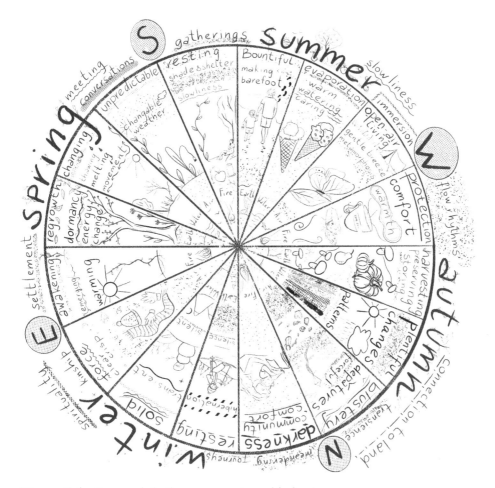

Figure 5.4   Seasonal rhythms, concepts and behaviours

When we explore concepts that exist in the natural world around us, we can create broad understandings of patterns, rituals and rhythms in day-to-day experiences. We can create environments that support this love of nature through biophilic design principles.

The décor and design of the indoor environment responds to the palette and forms of the natural world:

- Lighting is natural as far as possible with low-energy systems in place.
- The materials are stone, wood, metal and glass.
- The design is home-like rather than institutional.
- The flow works across three locations of inside, outside and beyond.

Learning through the land – integrated design, adventure, discordant, security, journeys

In the initial chapters of this book, we explored what nature is and how we can truly be in relation with it. When we learn through the land, we are consciously aware of our place on the Earth and how there is a synergy we can become aware of that exists between humans and the rest of the natural world. It is not always harmonious, but in the discordant moments we can develop a sense of security that we are all on a journey along with everything else on the planet.

- The integration of inside-out means that the ceiling and carpet changes every day as unexpected wonders appear and disappear.
- The design of the outdoor area is driven by the children's voices and behaviours as they respond to the space itself.
- The landscape is in a continual state of change as it invites children to go on adventures physically and metaphorically.
- The dynamic need to respond to unexpected moments makes the natural environment challenging, discordant and supportive all at the same time.
- Learning through the land offers a sense of rhythm and security that is not available in the virtual world. The adults and children are supported to have a problem-solving, can-do attitude that affects the way that children embrace challenge in their play and explorations.
- Learning journeys are seen to be valuable in terms of all aspects of human flourishing that embraces intellectual, physical, emotional and spiritual development. Growing as humans places us in the company of other living things.

Holistic experiences – freedom, exploration, inquiry, authentic, relevant

The principles and practice stem from the philosophy that the parts of something are interconnected and explicable only by reference to the whole. This educational ideology is rooted in the philosophy that we are all connected in an unobservable meshwork (Ingold, 2011).

This drives us to be sustainable in all aspects of the word, from reducing plastic and use of power, all the way to small moments such as stopping at the entrance of the forest and listening to birdsong or noticing the beauty of flowers as acknowledgement of the relationship. These moments offer the opportunity for adults to use participatory language such as 'we' rather than 'it', and relational phrases such as 'what a gift today, the sun is shining and everything in the forest feels awake'.

Holistic learning offers children a sense of intellectual freedom that embraces all the dispositions for learning, curriculum outcomes in encounters that are unpredictable and complex.

Figure 5.5 Dialogue and pedagogy come together to support growth in thinking

- Hands-on exploration engages the mind and body to learn concepts and skills before they are narrowly defined.
- Learning is concept led and inquiry based, with learning pathways defined by adults and children together.
- Authentic, real-world contexts and materials support children to make a link between what they know and have experienced, and new ideas and theories.
- Relevancy comes through empowerment. Children drive their learning whilst being challenged and stimulated by the environment.
- Respect is modelled for all things, from the plants to the insects, to each other as humans.

Place based – culture, connection, identity

The natural environment is viewed in terms of aspects such as geology, ecology, culture and how they are presented in the design itself and the curricula it supports; the child, family and carers, elders and ancient communities, and the land on which the setting stands are represented in the setting. The focus is to support the unique rather than the generic.

- The site provides a location, but the community creates the place. The cultural capital expands as people, culture and environment work together as a collective.
- Having pride in and a connection with a place is demonstrated through care and appreciation of everything, from a warm day to a beautiful flower to a china bowl.
- Identity comes through a feeling that you belong, that you are involved and that you can see things in the space that resonate with you. The changing shed is an important part of outdoor practice in Scotland as the weather is often wet.

The operational challenge was the varying levels of self-help skills in the group, so the children, staff and families created a sensory area in one end of the change shed using wooden offcuts, upcycled materials from old nails and a water bottle. Nature-based play is often portrayed as leading to messy and unkempt environments and yet it can also manifest as care, pride and precision with a strong sense of identity.

Participatory – voice, rights, theories, plans, ideas and long term

The adult engages children in a pedagogical dance that allows movement of the power balance between the roles of leader and follower. When this happens, a more balanced, participatory ethos can develop.

- The behavioural boundaries are negotiated and explained, but once set, are asserted by the adults.
- The planning and programming practices involve and empower children to be heard in the planning and decision making of the setting in partnership with the adults.
- The voice of the child, parent and carer entwine with the educators as they create learning pathways within the curriculum to create connections.

Figure 5.6   Sensory waiting area in the change shed

- Pathways and adventures hold lines of inquiry that are trans- and inter-curricular so the child can choose which pathway to follow to support greater participation.
- This process of participation is gentle and slow, so the ideas and their inherent learning are formulated over time that works in pace with the natural world. Inquiries can take a year to complete or are sometimes re-explored over several years to bring out annual changes in the natural world.
- The right to be heard is manifested through the Floorbook® approach, which is built on documenting children's voices through their ideas and theories.
- Children have a right to be both heard and consulted. The group documentation links the learning inside, outside and beyond.
- Children's ideas, plans and theories are at the heart of the planning cycle.
- The adult is a co-creator in the space and holds an intentional view to offer opportunities in response to children's fascinations.
- Floorbooks® hold the memories of adventures and experiences to support reflective practice with children, families, and practitioners.
- The planning and documentation work in nature time and therefore can last over seasons, or indeed years, for children to look back at experiences on the site and come to feel and notice the rhythms of the land. In the image in Figure 5.7, the children tried to solve the problem of which

bird had made a nest they had found in the garden area. The abandoned nest was taken inside and the model eggs and the ID cards (made by the adults) supported children to explore numbers of eggs, size and dimension linked to the local birds.

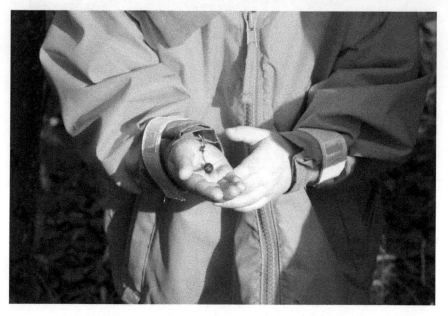

Figure 5.7   Children develop their own theories about the natural world

Inclusive and rights focused – rights, listen, share, sensitivity, expectation and care

The natural world is inclusive, and as such, it sends clear implicit messages to all children about their role in the community of the setting. The whole environment follows the concept of making 'human sense'. This supports curiosity and discourse about individualism within a role of community.

- Children are individuals who collectively create community with their families and staff. Bias is spoken about openly, as the natural world does not carry an agenda – it treats all children the same.
- Sensitive interactions and adaptations allow all children the opportunity to engage.
- Professional care and love are demonstrated through being aware of and sensitive to the emotional needs of the children and colleagues. Love is demonstrated by the adults in a caring way, offering to help another, caring

to enquire how somebody is feeling, being empathetic, caring for the animals and plants on the site.

- There is a clear expectation of inclusive behaviours. Adults are encouraged to be physically low down to be accessible to children, and adapt their interaction to support all children to engage.

Ecocentric – sustainable, living values, balance, food, lighting, power, transport

Humans are viewed as integral parts of the natural world, and as such, practice sustainability for themselves and the planet.

- The natural world and our place in it are equal so there is a daily focus on seeking balance.
- Nature pedagogy is a sustainable way of living and learning that supports children to flourish. It develops the capacities for a lifestyle that works with the rest of the natural world in a sustainable way for the planet and us as organisms on it.
- Our values guide our practice, and the natural world shares its space with us for the site, contexts, fascinations and resources.
- Conscious decisions are made around the sustainable aspects in Chapter 6 that will benefit the following generations.

Riskful – emotional, social, physical, intellectual and spiritual

In Chapter 3, we explored the perception of hazards and risk taking as a physical concept. Pushing boundaries needs to occur in all aspects of our growth as human beings in society.

- Pushing boundaries across all areas enables children to challenge themselves across all areas of their development.
- The benefit of the risk assessment process is used to consider the impact, procedures and behaviours that nature pedagogues use (see Chapter 7). All types of risk taking are supported as children develop greater understanding about their identity.
- The nurturing space allows open conversations whilst providing negotiated boundaries for group behaviours in order to maintain the peace.

Spiritual – unobservable, observable, relationships, living, non-living

Being with nature in spirit, discussed in Chapter 4, touched on the many ways that people consider that there is a phenomenon that is present when we open ourselves to the possibility. The sense of being part of something bigger has supported many people to have a sense of purpose in their lives, which is seen in the desire to assume the status of protector of nature. It could in fact be the reverse.

- The desire to be with the rest of the natural world is acknowledged and celebrated.
- This sense provides the conditions for stillness, being and mindfulness as part of the daily process, rather than as a defined activity.
- There is an acknowledgement by the adults that the experiences reside in the more-than-human realm.
- There are moments that are silent, where children experience slow relational encounters.
- These calm, peaceful moments support emotional literacy, social awareness and a sense of spirit.

If children are to feel comfortable with all the facets of the natural world, then the adults can model how to accept the possibility that it is both observable and unobservable.

Unique – curious, energetic, thoughtful, caring, dynamic, inquisitive

Children have a right to be in contact with the rest of the natural world in urban and rural locations. Sustainability is at the heart of the philosophy, in so far as we believe that we need to consider the values and priorities that children develop. This ensures that we need a balance between the health of the planet and the generation we leave for it. There are three frameworks that we embrace in our nature pedagogy at Auchlone Nature Kindergarten in our day-to-day practice. The first is that our practice and site development is guided by the United Nations' 17 Sustainable Development Goals (United Nations, 2015); the United Nations Convention on the Rights of the Child (UNCRC; United Nations, 1990), which guides the wider practices of the setting; and the land is accorded rights in line with the World Charter (1982) by us as tenants if not legally by the landowners. Part of the advocacy programme of this work in nature pedagogy is to support a sense of empowerment and activism, such as adding a child's right to nature to be included in the UNCRC.

- Children are full of curiosity, energy and love, which is embraced in the type of experiences.
- They flourish when they play and learn with the dynamic and unpredictable natural world.
- Each child is welcomed as an individual but is supported to be thoughtful and aware of the needs of both the human and the rest of the natural world around them.
- The sense of thoughtfulness comes from the management role all the way through to the adults and the children.

All humans are part of the natural world; it is full of variety and complexity, and as such, is the starting point for being with children in authentic ways. This means that if children are interested in milk, they visit a cow; if that is not possible, they go to the store and buy many kinds of milk so that they can engage materially with the subject. They might make cheese, or milkshakes, or study the range of local cows and use their real names. This real, immersive experience allows for conversations around diversity and inclusivity as all aspects of the natural world, not just selected perfection, are presented in secondary sources.

CONSIDER

How can you create a joint vision for nature pedagogy in your setting?

Which words resonate with you in the values and principles graphic (Figure 5.3) that could be part of your own value set?

Which of the principles connected to you and why?

Arts-based training is unusual as part of pedagogical thinking. How could you use it in your situation to open dialogue?

Nature pedagogy is driven by the values and principles noted in this chapter, and thought is given towards the way that they impact practice in the day-to-day aspects of the environment offered by the natural world but also shaped and presented by humans. Team cohesion and understanding influences all the small decisions and choices we make every day when we work with children. When all these small elements are guided by broader values and principles, the quality of ecocentric provision increases and nature pedagogy can flourish.

SUMMARY

- Nature pedagogy is a value-driven practice that centralises the natural world in the decisions and choices that are made.
- Values are linked to our inner beliefs and these need to be explored through dialogue to explore bias and subtle discrimination that we may have developed through our own lives.
- The creation and development of values and principles take time, but are key to long-term sustainability in nature pedagogy.
- Ecocentric values and principles are positional in that they respond to climate, culture, curriculum and community.

Six

Sustainability as an approach to care and education

Chapter overview

This chapter explores the areas of green education or eco-pedagogy and the growing awareness of the ecosystem that we are part of; wild pedagogies and kinship in terms of learning about, in, with and for the natural world, as we explore how we support ourselves and work with children in a way that is sustainable for the planet and us.

One of the key purposes of this book is to create links between research, theory and practice, so the infographics in the figures provide an overview of some of the many moments that can be embedded in our day-to-day experiences with children.

Human impact, including climate change, biodiversity loss, extinct and endangered species and contamination of environments have been put forward as evidence that we are entering a stage in our evolution defined by the scientist Paul Crutzen as the 'Anthropocene'.

Taylor and Pacini-Ketchbaw (2015: 509) call 'into question the sustainability of life on earth as we know it, including the survival of our own species'. We must change our approach and find a place to start, which is within reach of all educators around the world and is the root of how we work with children and families – our pedagogy. As noted, nature pedagogy (Warden, 2018) has been defined as the art of being in relation with nature inside, outside and beyond in observable and unobservable ways. When this is intertwined with philosophies of co-construction and a view of the child as full of agency, it becomes sustainable as a pedagogical approach to early years education.

Ecocentric education focuses on intrinsic values of the ecosystem, environment and individual living beings. To achieve this goal globally, we need to embrace a nature pedagogy that orientates our thinking away from ourselves as supreme (ego pedagogy) to a more integral, relational pedagogy (eco pedagogy).

Education for sustainability in the early years may take more time, but there is evidence that young children are capable of comprehending sustainable education principles (Davis and Elliott, 2014). However, there are many situations and many models of early years provision, as noted in Chapter 4, and not all centralise the place of sustainability for the natural world. In the USA, curricula positions the environment as a backdrop for children to act upon: to care for, to save, to experience, rather than to work towards transformational change more holistically for the environment (Ginsburg and Audley, 2002). Given that USA pre-schools (for children aged three/four years) are primarily academically focused on pre-literacy and numeracy skills (Tobin et al., 2009), it would require a strategic policy shift to make widespread change. Nature-based early years could be an exception if there is a positive engagement with nature pedagogy. In the USA, these programmes often embed sustainability education into curricula, but *how* they plan and deliver the concepts may still be adult directed. In addition to the more traditional subjects of language, literacy, mathematics, and social-emotional development, these nature-based pre-school programmes often spend a significant part of the day outdoors (Larimore, 2016). However, as noted earlier, being outside may not be enough to develop ecocentric values and beliefs, which may reside in relationships.

Agency and activism

Everyone can become an agent for change, challenging practices through educational innovation. The challenge we have in society is referred to as intergenerational environmental amnesia (Kahn and Kellert, 2002: 348). If each generation uses their experience of nature as the benchmark, the reference point changes to be indifferent to environmental impact and losses as they have no memory of what it once was. Mary Pipher, in her book *The Shelter of Each Other*, describes a lifestyle that is very familiar to an increasing number of young children all over the world: 'Many children today find it easier to stay indoors and watch television. I worry that children do not know what they are missing. Children cannot love what they do not know. They cannot miss what they have not experienced' (Pipher, 2008: 32).

The foundation of ecocentric thinking isn't a new fundamental concept, as it emerges from First Nation thinking. What is innovative is the way it is applied through nature pedagogy in today's contexts, theorised in current research and shared by a growing number of educators who are seeking educational innovation in their own practice so that the natural world is embedded in their pedagogy, not peripheral to it.

In days gone by, there was a real connection to rhythms and cycles beyond and within the year where the adult and child worked together, as shown in the previous chapter, where language and the natural world were intertwined. William Bird once said that 'what we have done is put nature over there – we have put a fence around it and said it's Nature. This is why we are now strangers to each other' (Moss, 2012: 28). The issue of sustainability doesn't sit with an age group or one location, but applies to a global society.

Sustainable behaviours have been explored with primary school children, but the early years may offer greater potential for child and adult pro-environmental behaviours as a collaboration through the ecocentric values shared in Chapter 5 (Chawla and Derr, 2012; Larson et al., 2011; Rosa et al., 2018).

Wherever you are on the globe, there will be something that heralds the passage of a point of change. As adults, we can be more mindful of this seasonal change, from the smallest point such as the arrival of visiting birds to the larger-scale issues of global climate change. This enables us to be aware of patterns, connections and relationships and our impact on them, as shared in Chapter 5, and make wiser choices that sustain the planet and therefore us as humans.

CASE STUDY

Food, shelter and community at Auchlone Nature Kindergarten

Being able to sustain good health is an integral part of the pattern of sustainability for future generations. The impact of pesticides on food, air pollution and the degradation of the materials they encounter cannot be ignored. As can be seen from Figure 6.1,

(Continued)

rituals and routines can feature in early years work and these include sourcing, preparing and eating food.

Children make bread every day. There are a variety of methods to choose from; for example, yeast based in the bread maker and simple unleavened bread for stick bread, whereas damper goes in the ash or into the Dutch oven in the embers of the fire. The sequence and connection to the food we eat is part of our value system, but it needs to be balanced with an impact on the environment and children of the smoke from the fire, the heat from the fire on the ground and the collection of wood. Wherever we go, we have an impact, so we need to think deeply about when or whether we need a fire, the design of the fire stands that keep the fire off the ground to avoid sterilising the soil and everything in it, and that there are only certain woods we can collect for us and that the rest is left for the other animals. The tokenistic use of fire as a fun activity needs to be placed within nature pedagogy to understand its impact.

Making food is a social experience. It builds relationships and provides a context for communication as the children chat over their own method of making bread or how many berries the group picked on the collective journey to forage.

The space in which we work to prepare our produce is important as it reflects the values of this approach. The environmental aspects are integrated into all of our activities so that any space whether inside or out has recycling bins; low-energy light bulbs or natural daylight; a solar-powered heater to provide warmth in the very coldest months; thermal clothing to actually reduce the need for external heat sources; sustainable materials such as willow that can be harvested and used on a cyclical basis; food from our garden is used within the kitchen; and the local, organic mobile shop comes to the setting once a week so that and the children can purchase seasonal fruit and vegetables.

The Kinder Kitchen is an open-fronted, log construction designed to replicate the experience of being around the kitchen table of a busy family home. It is designed to be used by children whilst they are still in their outdoor suits if necessary. The design has an outdoor kitchen area with a surface at different levels to cater for the heights of children.

The creation of a real sense of place takes time. Aprons are made by children; clay plates are made, fired and glazed. The enamel mugs and real knives and forks are used to set the table. A gift from nature sits in the centre of the table to provoke conversation. On most days, the candles are lit and children and adults share lunch together. The atmosphere is not hurried and is treated as core teaching time so is planned with intent. Children are able to engage in eudaimonistic views of wellbeing (Huta and Waterman, 2014), which go beyond the need to feel happiness (hedonistic) to a place where wellbeing is experienced when doing things for others.

Although there is a call for more dynamic, bold approaches in education that unsettle people's understanding of the issues around sustainability, there are also many small moments that lead to a sense of empowerment, agency and ultimately, activism. Wrapped around the daily routines of life sit simple opportunities that hold the possibilities to develop ecocentric values that may lead to this deeper sense of wellbeing. These examples show how actions and values are linked. Values are noted in brackets.

- The uncooked, unsalted vegetable waste goes into the wormery or into the composting barrel (care, understanding of sharing, awareness of waste).

- Flowerpots are handmade from newspaper not bought in plastic (decomposition, human choices, materials, tending, care).
- The management of the garden is designed to minimise water loss and embraces permaculture seen through companion planting, drip feed systems, and small-scale hydroponics (relationships, benefits of diversity, value of water).
- Use of water in play is limited in the warm weather and water at the end of the day is used by children to water plants (awareness of the value of water, care).

The way that the garden space gives us produce is only one of its features, as the wonderment of simple living, together and sustainably, offers a basis for an inquiry into acres of land or a small hard-core play area, focused on relationships rather than quantity of produce. We will explore more of this way of planning for possibilities in Chapter 7.

Sustainability runs through everything we do, as Jickling said: 'creating educational experiences that are held, felt and disruptive might just be the basis for learning that is indeed transformational' (Jickling, 2017: 28).

Not everything about a societal shift can be laid at the feet of access to technology. Indeed, our perception of the elitism of knowledge has changed as we can all access film, images and text where the devices exist. What has evolved is the flexibility of taking a screen with us, which can serve as a distraction to the real experience; conversely, it also allows us to hold a memory and share it more widely, so perhaps the key focus should be balancing time with and without a screen.

The impact of childhood consumerism has led to the sense of making it necessary to 'equip' them with every manner of toy from plastic bears to rubber pizza. If we *trust* the play affordances of the loose materials that nature provides, we can offer a basket of stones and pebbles in the math area in the sure knowledge that children will count and sort them; if we *see* the natural beauty of real materials, we will provide skeleton leaves on a light table and plants in the book corner; if we *are aware* of the sensitive nature of children's vision, we will give them many shades of green, not just one; if we *understand* the sensorial complexity of nature, we will allow children to create small worlds inside with real grass trays, twig fences and stone walls; if we *believe* in the calming effect of nature, we will put leaves in the sand tray to simply handle; when we believe in the holistic nature of connecting to nature, we will allow children to watch a candle burn as they eat their snack and reflect on their time outside, as they sit in the comfortable knowledge that nature has been invited into all aspects of their care and education. When we work with children, we are using experience to build up threads of consciousness that create a framework of values, but these values need to be applied and so they go hand in hand with activism, agency and empowerment of children's voices.

—————————————————— **CONSIDER** ——————————————————

Using the sustainability graphics in Figure 6.1, how can you embed these rituals into the setting?

How can nature pedagogies be developed to move beyond a list of things to do to help sustainable practices, towards sustainable care and education?

The United Nations 17 Sustainability Goals guide planetary decisions. The image in Figure 6.1 shows the elements of a sustainable programme with some of the things we can do every day as part of our routines that stem from social, economic and environmental sustainability.

The detail of how you can make an impact on these in practice is offered here as three overview graphics (Figure 6.2) with the understanding of the interrelationship. They will be most effective when children are actively involved in the decision making, and work is taken across boundaries of the setting and the community.

Figure 6.1   Overview of sustainable practices

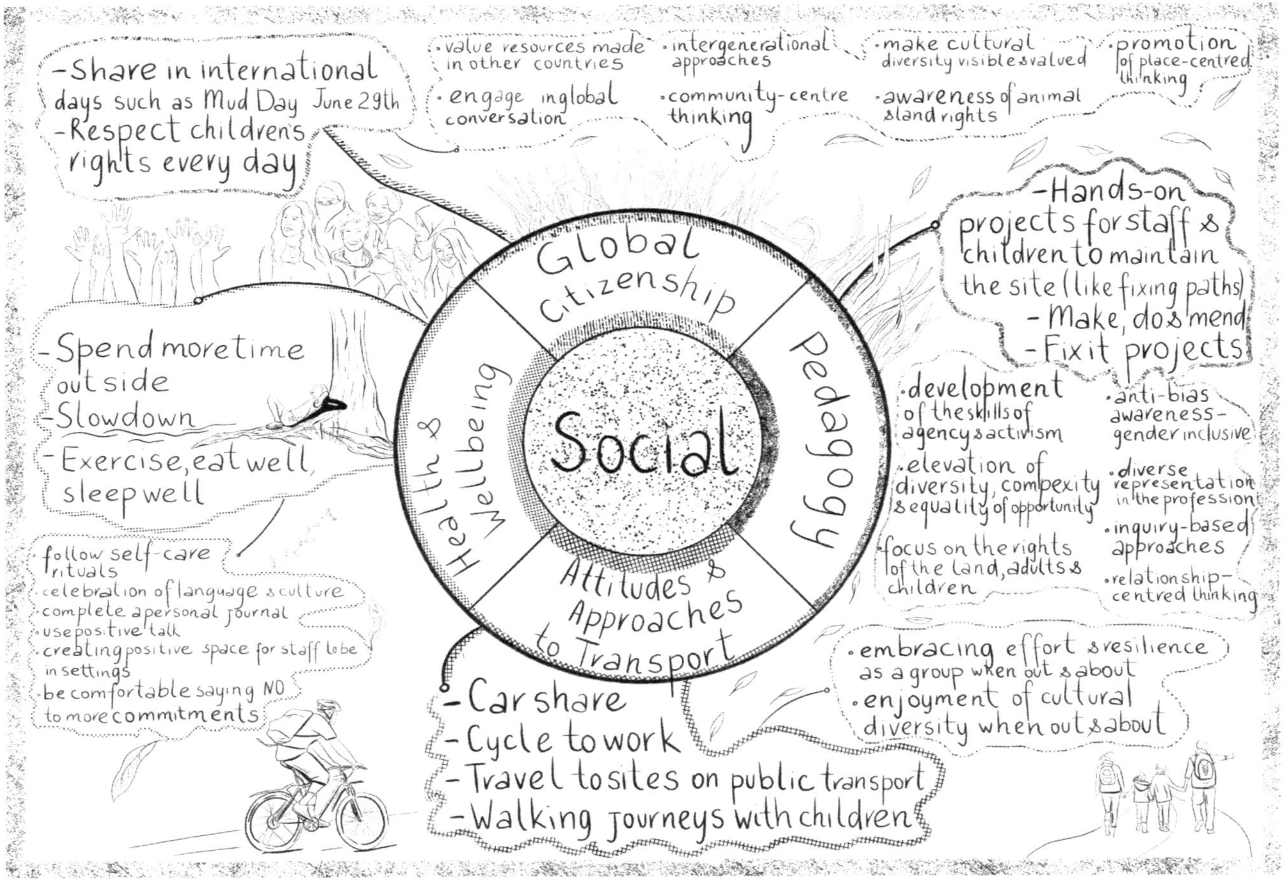

Figure 6.2 Social and cultural sustainability

The central circle reads: **Social**

Surrounding ring sections: **Pedagogy**, **Global Citizenship**, **Health & Wellbeing**, **Attitudes & Approaches to Transport**

Pedagogy (upper right cluster):
- development of the skills of agency & activism
- elevation of diversity, complexity & equality of opportunity
- focus on the rights of the land, adults & children
- anti-bias awareness – gender inclusive
- diverse representation in the profession
- inquiry-based approaches
- relationship-centred thinking

Hands-on projects cluster:
- Hands-on projects for staff & children to maintain the site (like fixing paths)
- Make, do & mend
- Fixit projects

Upper left cluster:
- make cultural diversity visible & valued
- promotion of place-centred thinking
- awareness of animal & land rights
- intergenerational approaches
- community-centre thinking

Left cluster (Global Citizenship):
- value resources made in other countries
- engage in global conversation
- Share in international days such as Mud Day June 29th
- Respect children's rights every day

Attitudes & Approaches to Transport cluster:
- embracing effort & resilience as a group when out & about
- enjoyment of cultural diversity when out & about
- Car share
- Cycle to work
- Travel to sites on public transport
- Walking journeys with children

Health & Wellbeing cluster (lower):
- Spend more time outside
- Slowdown
- Exercise, eat well, sleep well
- follow self-care rituals
- celebration of language & culture
- complete a personal journal
- use positive talk
- creating positive space for staff to be in settings
- be comfortable saying NO to more commitments

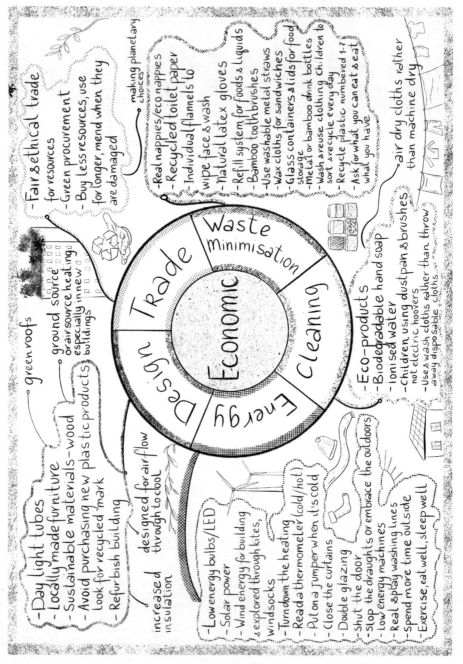

Figure 6.3 Economic sustainability

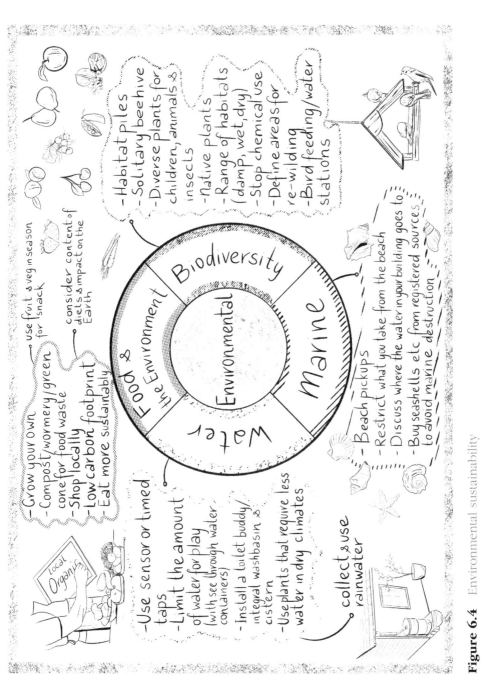

Figure 6.4 Environmental sustainability

Wild pedagogies

'Wild pedagogies' is the phrase used by Jickling et al. (2018) to engage practitioners in reclaiming, reimaging, and reintroducing them to education as a change agent in the field of sustainability and wider ecological awareness. As a concept, wild pedagogies is intended to challenge 'dominant cultural ideas about control – of each other, of nature, of education, and of learning' (Jickling et al., 2018: 3). Part of its strength is the inclusion of the practitioner directly in the experience so that they examine their relationship with their own pedagogical beliefs and values. This follows on from the desire to disrupt and disharmonise our thinking in order to help us challenge our own anthropocentric bias, as discussed in Chapters 2 and 3. In this work, there is a focus on long-term journeys that include touchstones as provocations to explore and revisit.

Jickling et al. (2018) relate to questions about wildness and control, about core elements that can be meaningful across disciplines and inclusive of the more-than-humans across ecosystems. They invite a different way of being in the world. Areas addressed by the six touchstones include:

1. agency and the role of nature as co-teacher
2. wildness and challenging ideas of control
3. complexity, the unknown and spontaneity
4. locating the wild
5. time and practice
6. cultural change.

When we consider the concept of touchstones with the team at Auchlone Nature Kindergarten, they challenge us to look deeply at the values, as shown in Chapter 5, and to embrace that they take time. The research for the team at Auchlone Nature Kindergarten was over two years, with the physical handling of wool, dyes, weaving and words to dig below the rhetoric of nature-based thinking.

Kinship

The International Environmental Kinship group has been working around concepts of emotional literacy and a deeper sense of relationship and connection with the natural world for several years. Through consultation with people from First Nation communities, environmental organisations, educational leaders and landscape designers we continue to explore the difference of contact and connection with the rest of the natural world. Its aim was to create a diagram and a practical framework to raise awareness of the interrelated perspective of the natural world that would enable clearer understanding and respect for divergent world views. The desire to create a bridge between reductionist views of nature-based thinking and those of more holistic approaches drove the group to consider the journey for practitioners when they are positioned in a context of little autonomy. The plethora of detailed guidelines and didactic curriculum activities for nature is in tension with a deeper, more holistic, understanding of our role and place in the natural world. The aspects of learning about, in, with and for the natural world have been explored earlier, but in this case, they drive forward the desire to create a sense of kinship across all humans and the other species we share the planet with.

The word 'kinship' has long been associated with close human relationships. Scots' language talks 'of kith and kin' to represent friends and relations; in Gaelic it is used in place names to denote the head of something such as a river. Kin is also of Germanic origin, from an Indo-European root meaning 'give birth to' and so it links to a blood relation. In many First Nation communities, kinship goes beyond a blood relation to be fundamental to social organisation. It is a complex system that determines how people relate to each other and their roles and responsibilities, and obligations in relation to one another, ceremonial business and land.

CONSIDER

In what ways does the word 'kinship' support you to consider the nature-based work you do?

Kinship is rooted in a deep kind of knowing that includes, but goes beyond, cognitive knowing. While the terms 'teaching' and 'learning' are often defined in relation to the acquisition of knowledge, they also refer to the development of understandings. Generating or gathering facts about the world around us is one way to know the world. Another way is to develop a relationship with it. 'To know' in this sense is 'to be aware of' or 'to be familiar with'. This type of knowing includes the realisation that humans and the rest of the natural world exist in relationship with each other (Fox et al., 2021).

In terms of the natural world, co-management of wildlife and landscapes often requires managers to work with Indigenous and conventional Western world views (Bhattacharyya and Slocombe, 2017). Many cultures recognise animals as non-human persons with decision-making agency. Such perspectives, termed 'kincentric ecology', suggest a relational approach to management that differs from convention in most parts of the world.

In relation to the graphic in Figure 6.5, an educational lens seeks to bring together four aspects of engaging with nature. Rather than separate threads of pedagogy, they are knotted together to show the interrelatedness of each aspect. All of the threads are connected and equally important as they weave

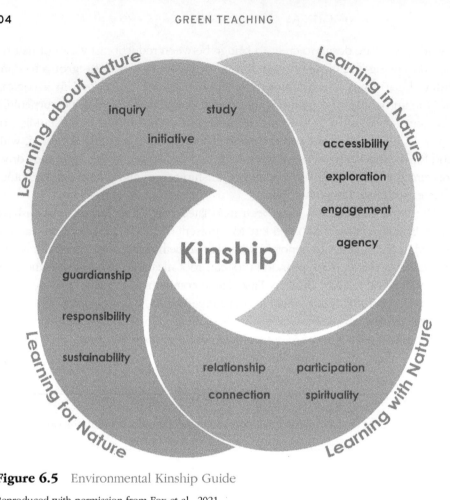

Figure 6.5   Environmental Kinship Guide

Reproduced with permission from Fox et al., 2021.

in and out of 'kinship'. For example, an *engagement* of recurrent time spent in nature may spark observations on leaf colour changes, which, in turn, instigates an *inquiry* in the changing of seasons. This inquiry may involve charting photographs throughout the year, which could then lead to a *spiritual* moment spent in wonder at the sight of snow covering their natural space, which could turn into a feeling of *responsibility* for that space. There is no particular order of engagement, as it happens organically and often feeds into other engagement styles.

The framework itself supports practitioners to notice what they see happening when they are with children and consider how they are portraying the natural world in their programmes, documentation and planning. The next chapter examines the implications for practice and how we transfer theory into our day-to-day actions.

SUMMARY

- Sustainable education and care can be explored through social and cultural, economic and environmental thinking.
- Ecocentric thinking supports ecosystems and is more likely to support flourishing of both the planet and the humans on it.
- When nature pedagogy incorporates inclusive, democratic strategies, such as Floorbooks®, an atmosphere of balance and mutual respect develops. This includes respect for the other elements, both living and non-living, on the planet.
- Children can be agentic and full of activism to act for the rest of the natural world if we give them the space and autonomy to take the lead.

Seven

Implications for practice

Chapter overview

The real value of educational research lies in the improvement of the quality of the lives of children. This chapter offers some implications of this green or ecocentric approach for practice in settings. Opportunities have arisen to think differently, to respond in bold innovative ways to create what people refer to as a 'new normal'. We explore how to embed this in all aspects of our work that will include defining and upholding a set of values, living and working sustainably in education, which includes how we document and plan with nature at the heart of the work we do so that we challenge the cycle of anthropocentric thinking.

Everyone is at a different place on the journey towards integrating ecocentric values into their work, so these suggestions are offered as points for consideration to develop your nature pedagogy.

Development of dynamic planning and programming

The first aspect is that nature pedagogy is defined as relational. It brings experiences together into ways that make human sense and therefore challenges some of the defined curricula that divide subjects and reduce them to component parts. This offers both a challenge to practice and an opportunity. The challenge is that nature pedagogy is holistic as it emerges from the integrated ecosystems in the natural world. So how can we as educators act as a bridge between reductionism and holism?

This challenge was the beginning of the work on planning with and for children through Floorbooks®. The responsive nature of this model of planning allows the agency and activism of children to come through very strongly, and makes programming and planning holistic and yet accountable to separate curricular outcomes.

Visual mind maps are drawn in conversation with children as part of the co-construction of the play and learning environment. These provocations are *possibility plans* as they offer children's own ideas as provocations for other children, unlike an adult thematic map, which is created by an adult and mapped out for children in a more rigid framework.

The combination of the consultative strategies within Floorbooks® and the natural world as a location, context and resource makes this particular nature pedagogy unique and yet universally applicable as it stems from working with the natural elements, as shown in Chapter 6 and later in this chapter.

The important aspect of this type of pedagogy is the skill and knowledge of the adult to look below the activity or experience into the fundamental main ideas or lines of inquiry (Warden, 1996). It is this pedagogical skill to make connections and see patterns in children's own playful inquiries that lies at the heart of being a nature pedagogue, as discussed later in this chapter. There are many ways that we can view the experiences of children – here are five that are taken from the learning journeys driven by children and documented within Floorbooks®.

The examples that follow show how some visual mind maps emerged from:

- a motivational context such as a den building
- through an adult lens of curricular content – pulling out the mathematics
- engagement with a material such as mud
- unexpected moments that occur outside from going on a walk
- concept-led inquiry.

These provide a wealth of materials to support children's ideas and choices but also provide evidence of intentional thinking by the adult.

Motivation and the inner drive to investigate are important to build in the engagement, especially when exploring how the outdoors can be embedded into the daily pressures that many six-year-olds encounter.

Through clear observation and the understanding of the theories of how children can be with nature, as noted in Chapter 4, we can follow their interests and consider the lines of inquiry that can be explored through following children's fascinations.

In many instances, the holistic nature of learning with nature is overtaken by the pressure to show accountability to separate curricular subjects such as language and mathematics. This summary of a learning journey took place over many weeks and supported the team to make the experiences visible through a lens of mathematical thinking. The process of self and peer evaluation can enable us to consider multiple perspectives, as described in the early chapters of this book.

The experiences noted in this book have shown how the four elements of earth, fire, air and water are used in the understanding of experiences and encounters. When we work with nature pedagogy, it becomes self-evident that we need to be far more aware of how the four elements offer us a location, a context and a resource.

To step below the surface of just being outside, to learning with it, the adult needs to understand materials and how they combine and work together in a variety of different ways. We can create a location for play such as a mud kitchen, but as we move further into understanding the possibilities of materials, we start to see that a mud kitchen is just one way to consider mud as a material, and actually, even in this space, has been reduced to a domestic interpretation rather than seeing how it could be used in an expansive and unlimited way. Creating a mud kitchen is a great space and place to start but should not be the end goal and, in some cases, has become just as commercialised and adult created as the indoor space. In nature pedagogy, as this book defines it, the material affords us many lines of inquiry that we can use to create endless play-based, but concept-led, inquiries.

If as practitioners we are to embrace the understandings of quantum biology and First Nation pedagogies, then every moment that we are outside and under the sky, we have the possibility that there will be a sense of something unobservable and observable around us. The visual mind map in Figure 7.4 shares the conversations that were afforded through the apparently simple moment of looking up when a group of children were on a walk.

The natural world is holistic, as we have discussed, and when we learn with it, we can experience its places, the contexts it affords us, the materials and the unexpected moments of simply looking. There is, however, a fifth way of approaching this thinking and that is through concept-led thinking.

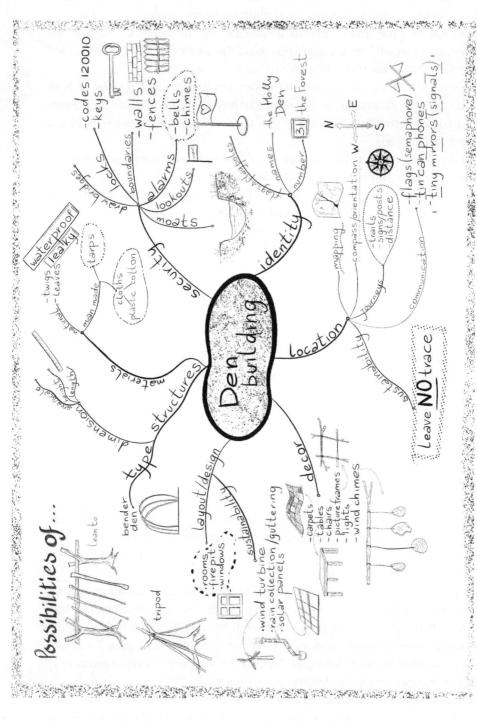

Figure 7.1 Visual mind map of the possibilities of a context such as den building

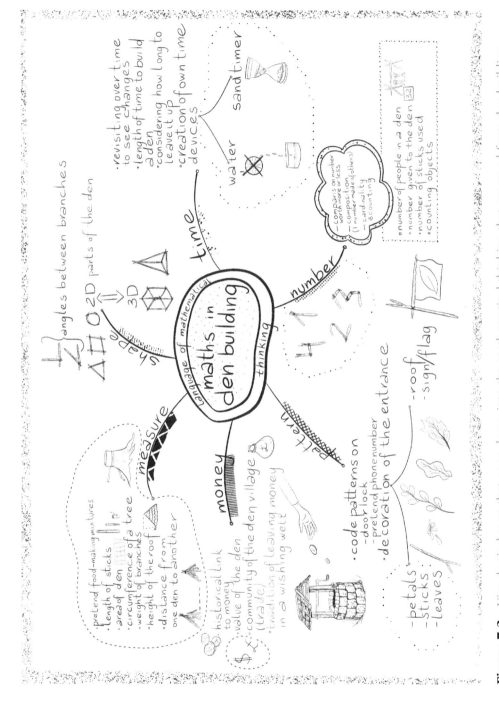

Figure 7.2 Visual mind map that goes down into the mathematical thinking that emerged from den building

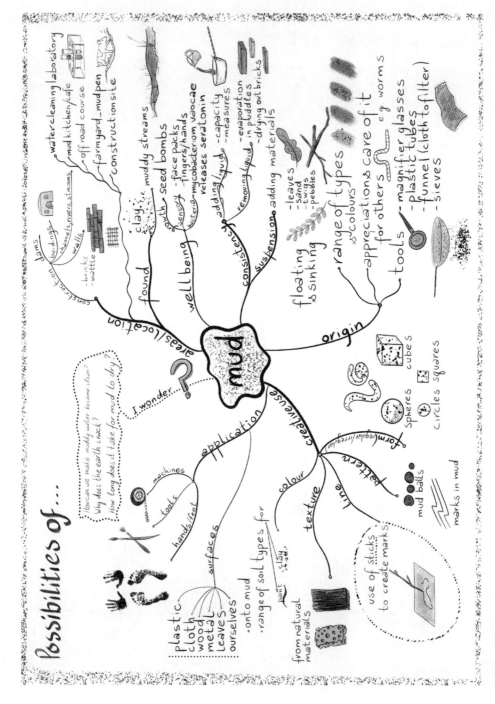

Figure 7.3 Visual mind map of the possibilities of a material: earth element – mud

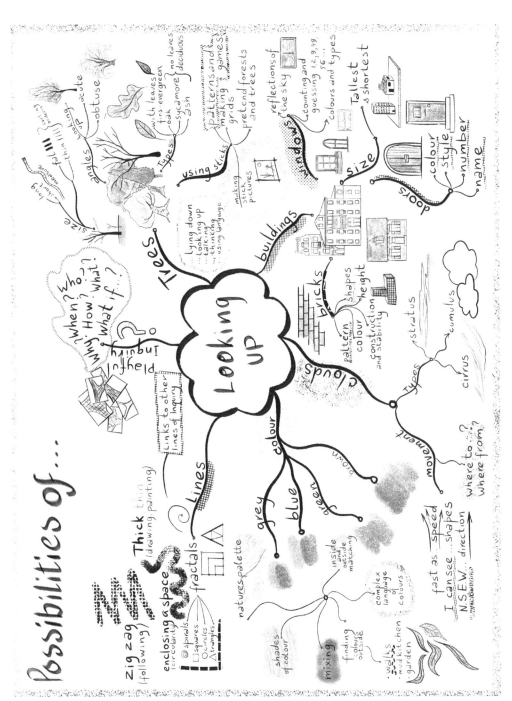

Figure 7.4 Visual mind map of the possibilities of unexpected moments of looking up

In the rituals and rhythms diagram in Chapter 5, concepts were linked to the elements of fire, earth, air and water. When we look at concepts, we can start to consider what is the essence of experiences and opportunities. For those of us in the UK, is autumn about making hedgehog pictures or a deeper understanding of the concept of resting, warmth and preparation? When we move from a narrow understanding of nature-based experiences as activities, we can begin to understand relationships and connections that children and adults are exploring in many instances almost without conscious awareness, as suggested in Chapter 3 in the exploration of quantum physics.

CONSIDER

In what ways could you consult children more so that your pedagogy and planning are more child led?

Do your requirements for planning drive your pedagogy rather than the other way around?

Development of holistic thinking

There are always challenges to the space and time that mainstream educators can protect for being outside the walls of a building, as detailed in the companion text to this book called *Learning with Nature – Embedding Outdoor Practice* (Warden, 2015). Green teaching or ecocentric pedagogies link rhythms like seasonal fluctuation, cycles of change in all the four elements of fire, earth, air and water, and includes humans. This pedagogy views the learning journey as being made up of cycles and loops rather than as single and linear. So, what impact does that have on our practice? The first is how we view the planning cycle, as noted earlier, but the second is to consider how we interact with children.

There is no one model of education or indeed a complete list of strategies that work effectively in the natural world, as noted earlier; it is a *totality of relationships* and therefore needs to embrace diversity of culture, climate, community and curriculum. The visual mind maps share possibilities of content but not *how* to be with children.

As nature pedagogues with value-driven practice, whatever you choose to do, or indeed, however you decide to be with children, it works well to:

• be responsive to the unexpected moments that both children and the natural world offer us
• respond to the range of weathers according to the climate where you work

- help children make connections and relationships between concepts/skills/ knowledge
- acknowledge the cultural diversity of the children and families in your care
- respect the places you go to
- support everyone to be aware that the natural elements have value beyond human benefit.

—————————————— CASE STUDY ——————————————

Holistic thinking about locations

In this example, we share some examples of how mapping out the uniqueness of the three spaces of inside the cottage, outside in the defined play area and beyond the gate into the wilder, more unpredictable spaces, enables us to consider how they link together.

This intentional and holistic framework of resources and strategies highlighted points of difference in *how* children experienced aspects of a curriculum in different ways, so the uniqueness of each space was preserved rather than making them all the same. This process of developing awareness supports teams to be with nature in a variety of ways and share the values, beliefs and principles noted in Chapter 5.

Aspect	Inside a building	Outside in a defined play area	Beyond the gate
Identity and entry	Welcome area/ reception Carpet areas in rooms A door A written and pictorial sign	Gathering place suggested by landscape e.g., positioning of a tree, boulder, bench, outdoor shelter, change of surface Area signage	A base camp suggested by the land - an elevation, a dip, a large tree, a flat area Acknowledgement and respect on entry to the space Traces - a pile of stones, a group of feathers in the earth, a named feature like the window tree

This intentionality in seeing the whole picture supports a rich and complex experience for children, and drives the adults in the space to consider the many aspects of relational thinking in their pedagogy.

—————————————— CONSIDER ——————————————

To what extent should we embed outdoor learning in everything that we do, or should it stay as a free outdoor space without planning and intent?

Should we be designing spaces that we let become wild, or do nature-based play spaces offer a transitional space for play from the built environment?

Development of professional status

The skills to embed nature pedagogy in practice have been considered historically through many cultural contexts. Many theorists have provided identities for
these adults, from rangers to pedagogues. This work within nature-based practice focuses on the professional who has more than an interest in being outside,
but has an holistic approach to the planetary and human benefits of being with
it in myriad different ways. They are driven by the values outlined in Chapter 5
and blend together an understanding of effective co-constructive pedagogy and
a deepening knowledge and awareness of the elements of the natural world.

As noted before, all theorists (especially those outside Europe) draw on the
totality of relationships to support children, and ultimately society, to be less
egocentric in their approaches, but strive to be ecocentric to benefit generations
into the future.

The time feels right to value the natural world and therefore people who find
a synergy with it as a location, context for inquiry and sustainable resource. The
following case study shares the work of a group of colleagues who explored the
concept of excellence in the professional role of nature pedagogue.

─────────── CASE STUDY ───────────

Qualities that define an excellent nature pedagogue

The European Region Action Scheme for the Mobility of University Students (ERASMUS)
project (2018) was set up by Anders Farstad (Norway), Claire Warden (Scotland), Sue Stoke
(England) and David Landspersky (Czech Republic). Despite the many observed curricular
and cultural differences across the four countries, the working group developed and agreed
seven pedagogical qualities that were present in their work. The research took place over
four years (2014-2018) and involved practitioners' exchange and mentoring sessions.

The seven qualities help practitioners to consider elements of their behaviour and
their importance in the work that they do. Many of the qualities interrelate and it is the
combination of these that are found in a nature pedagogue.

When rethinking the qualities that an adult needs to have to work in the field of
nature pedagogy, it is useful to explore the qualities or traits that appear to make a difference. More can be found and studied in the footage from the settings, best practice
videos and interviews of headteachers, managers and nature pedagogues, which are
available at www.livingclassrooms.org.uk.

1. **Reflective**
   - Engaged in the cycle of reflection: facts, feelings, findings and future
     (Greenaway, 1992).
   - Uses child-centred planning, observation and assessment.

- Welcomes peer observation and support.
- Effective at self-assessment.
- Offers a supportive relationship.
- Looks internally, externally and beyond at who they are.

2. **Open not dominant**
   - Responsive to child-led learning.
   - Not directive.
   - Without fixed outcomes – still with intention, but open to opportunity.
   - Follows an interest, irrespective of time.
   - Has open body language – at the child's level, with eye contact.
   - Allows the child to lead.
   - When not teaching a specific skill set, learns together with the children.
   - Encourages children to self-assess/problem solve.
   - Really listens to the child's 'voice'.
   - Knows when to interact and not interfere.
   - Inclusive of alternative thoughts and ideas of children.
   - Accepts that children's thoughts do not always follow the intended line of inquiry.

3. **Happy and secure outside**
   - Positively connects to the outdoors.
   - Fully engages in real interactions.
   - Demonstrates calm and comfort.
   - Dresses appropriately for weather conditions.
   - Has confidence in own skills and knowledge to feel secure in an outdoor environment.

4. **Skills and knowledge (skill set)**
   - Understands the theory of nature-based pedagogy.
   - Has experience of being with nature.
   - Knows the individual child well.
   - Learns through exploration (adult and child), applying knowledge appropriately.
   - Develops skills for appropriate intervention.
   - Knows when and how to use own knowledge to teach specific skills.
   - Motivated for self-development.
   - Relevant skills and knowledge vary in each country/culture.
   - Good interpersonal skills.

5. **Respectful**
   - Wants to get to know children/colleagues as individuals.
   - Has their own respect and care of nature/environment.
   - Respectful to the children's play spaces and their property.

(Continued)

- Asks permission before action.
- Uses the skills of compromise/agree/discuss.
- Allows children to solve or attempt to solve own conflicts before stepping in.
- Thanks others for thoughts, ideas and help.
- Helps others to understand their place in nature.
- Values the rights of the child in everything they do.

6. **Synergy with nature**

Defined as an interaction of elements that, when combined, produces an effect greater than some individual parts.

- Don't overtake from nature; we have a balance of taking and giving.
- The setting will add value to the community, changing thoughts of the service users.
- Learning with nature, not just teaching about it.
- Following the seasons/elements.
- Complete cycle from start to finish (making charcoal, fishing, observing frogspawn to frogs).
- Learning contrasts: being cold and knowing how to get warm.
- Working with the environment, not against it - not always sticking to the plan (for example, still making kites even though it's a sunny calm day, just because it's in the planning).

7. **Collaboration**

Defined as strong teamwork, where the team members support each other to make learning with and in nature work.

- Recognising that it often takes a combined effort to achieve goals.
- Knowing the power of collaboration and when to use it in practice.
- Using individual strengths to reach the team's full potential.
- Negotiations and compromises that involve the voices of all.
- Sharing good practice with others across regions, countries, and so on.
- Being intuitive with colleagues.
- Trusting other colleagues.
- Forming strong relationships with colleagues, children and families.
- Effective leadership that manages collaboration.

CONSIDER

How do you define the qualities that are needed in a nature pedagogue?

Which qualities are vital to working with the natural world?

Increase global accessibility

The research has shown that there is a difference in opportunity to access larger areas of green landscaping. However, within nature pedagogy the core elements allow us to consider the potential of something as simple as a shadow or a drop of water. Thinking in this way crosses postcodes and different cultural and societal values to be inclusive.

It seems bizarre to consider that technology could be another way forward to make a collective difference to the lives of children in relation to connecting to the natural world, but it may well be part of the solution. An example of this beyond a practitioner meshwork was shared in a project by Living Classrooms CIC (community interest company) who developed an international Virtual Nature School, which embraced technology in a positive way.

———————————— CASE STUDY ————————————

Virtual Nature School

In March 2020, when the impact of the Covid-19 pandemic became apparent, we had no vision of what our work would look like a year later. Bravo Nyamudoka and I decided to offer support at home for children and families using the natural world as the context, location and resource. Although it seemed that there was a tension between virtual worlds and the physicality of nature, it became apparent that it was the relationships that were built, conversations that were had and experiences that were offered as choices that created a passionate motivation and drive in families, children and practitioners. The digital world, with its ability to bring the natural world into every home with technology, allowed greater accessibility and equality of opportunity.

The use of simple film provocations to inspire rather than direct allowed children's voices to come through in the planning and creation of the programme called Virtual Nature School. Children joined in the meetings from all over the world and created their own meshwork, linking families with the same values, engaging in home-based education or in hubs for the children of key workers. These free provocation films can still be accessed through the Virtual Nature School YouTube channel.

With Scottish Government funding, Virtual Nature School evolved to suit the needs of the children, families and early years practitioners. The first iteration was as a group of children, the second worked with families and practitioners, and the third focused more on practitioners and supported them in being nature-based practitioners through inquiry-based pedagogies.

The impact was that in over a year, more than 40,000 children were reached and there was 100 per cent feedback that confidence to be with children outside and

(Continued)

engage with the natural elements had increased. The aspect that had the greatest impact was the sense of awareness, agency and activism that practitioners felt they had been supported to develop, not a list of ideas.

CONSIDER

How do you balance the digital and physical approach in relation to nature-based pedagogies?

The drive to go deeper into our pedagogy reflects the professional passion to understand how it is that we can learn with the natural world in a more integral way. It moves us beyond simple locations for play such as *the outdoors*, away from single models such as forest school, to an area where we can debate as international colleagues how we can develop the understanding of a meshwork of equivalence. This will support the development of the many thousands of ways that we can engage with the rest of nature, which will in turn help the planet and ultimately ourselves. The International Association of Nature Pedagogy (www. naturepedagogy.com) was developed with this in mind, devolving the concept of knowledge from a few to many, and acknowledges the principles noted in Chapter 5. It thrives on the fact that activism and agency are traits that are desirable in both children and adults.

SUMMARY

- There are many aspects of educational practice that prevent practitioners from going outside. Pedagogy is one very important aspect that needs to be addressed.
- Moving away from anthropocentric thinking to ecocentric thinking will require adults to be open to new possibilities to address the balance of power in their work.
- Child-led inquiry, documentation and planning as seen in Floorbooks® and Talking Tubs share the possibilities for playful learning.
- Responsive, dynamic and creative ways to be with children outside will allow the unpredictable, complex opportunities to be embedded in our nature pedagogy.

In conclusion

A chapter on the implications for practice could be endless as we all take different things from what we read. If there were key things that we could do to embrace nature pedagogy in our work it would be to, first, push ourselves to challenge our own ontology (world view). Our view of the world has become egocentric, and in doing so, it has broken down many of the relationships that are needed for a healthy planet, such as clean air, uncontaminated water and areas of refuge for animals.

Secondly, we should feel and embrace the discomfort of acknowledging what we have done and still do, and then use that as a starting point to disrupt the expected to develop more ecocentric practices. In education, that means changing the way we work with children so that they understand the holism and balance in all their relationships, whether looking up at the sky, playing with mud or building a den.

Thirdly, we need to accept the uncertain such as the domain of spirituality, which is an unobservable space whether through a lens of quantum physics or through First Nation thinking. It is time to consider words that resonate with us and link them to multiple ways of knowing that are emotive and unmeasurable in the quantifiable research. We feel comfortable with love as a human emotion, but are we ready intellectually to accept a two-way, unobservable link between all things in an ecosystem that include us?

Lastly, we need to hold on to our professional identity and move as a collective to make a difference with the children we work with every day, and push expectations of what a group of professionals identifying as nature pedagogues could achieve around the world. People often say, 'it's all been done before'. Well, if it has, it didn't work. So let us try in our time, to be bold, be innovative and think outside the box, to embed a form of green teaching in the widest sense to make a more sustainable pedagogy for the planet and us.

Bibliography

Please note that single first names are used in response to the wishes of First Nation peoples.

Al-Khalili, J. (2014) *The Secrets of Quantum Physics: Let There Be Life.* [part two of a two-part documentary]. BBC Four. Retrieved on 10 March 2022 from https://www.youtube.com/watch?v=ain8eyqQ3M4.

Al-Khalili, J. and McFadden, J. (2014) *Life on the Edge: The Coming of Age of Quantum Biology.* Kindle edition. London: Transworld Digital.

Altman, I. and Rogoff, B. (1987) 'World views in psychology: trait, interactional, organismic and transactional perspectives', in D. Stokols and I. Altman (eds), *Handbook of Environmental Psychology*, vol. 1, pp. 7–40. Hoboken, NJ: John Wiley & Sons.

Ärlemalm-Hagsér, E. (2013) *An Interest in the Best for the World? Education for Sustainability in the Swedish Preschool.* Doctoral thesis, Gothenburg Studies in Educational Sciences 335. Gothenburg: Acta Universitatis Gothoburgensis.

Askwith, R. (2014) *Running Free: A Runner's Journey Back to Nature.* London: Yellow Jersey Press.

Aspinall, P., Mavros, P., Coyne, R. and Roe, J. (2013) 'The urban brain: analysing outdoor physical activity with mobile EEG', *British Journal of Sports Medicine*, 49 (2): 272–76. DOI: 10.1136/bjsports-2012-091877.

Bateson, G. (1979) *The Mind and Nature: A Necessary Unity.* New York: Dutton.

Bhattacharyya, J. and Slocombe, S. (2017) 'Animal agency: wildlife management from a kincentric perspective', *Ecosphere*, 8 (10).

Bird-David, N. (1992) 'Beyond "the original affluent society": a culturalist reformulation', *Current Anthropology*, 33: 25–47.

Bragg, R. (2013) *Measuring Connection to Nature in Children Aged 8–12: A Robust Methodology for the RSPB.* Colchester: University of Essex.

Bronfenbrenner, U. and Morris, P. A. (1998) 'The ecology of developmental processes', in W. Damon and M.A. Lerner (eds), *Handbook of Child Psychology, Vol. 1: Theoretical Models of Human Development*, 5th edn, pp. 993–1023. Hoboken, NJ: John Wiley & Sons.

Brosterman, N. (2002) *Inventing Kindergarten.* New York: Harry N. Abrams, Inc.

Brown, D., Barton, J. and Gladwell, V. (2013) 'Viewing nature scenes positively affects recovery of autonomic function following acute mental stress', *Environmental Science and Technology*, 47 (11): 5562–9.

Bruner, J. (1996) *The Culture of Education*. Cambridge, MA: Harvard University Press.

Brussoni, M., Gibbons, R., Gray, C., Ishikawa, T., Sandseter, E.B.H., Bienenstock, A., Chabot, G., Fuselli, P., Herrington, S., Janssen, I., Pickett, W., Power, M., Stanger, N., Sampson, M. and Tremblay, M. (2015) 'What is the relationship between risky outdoor play and health in children? A systematic review', *International Journal of Environmental Research and Public Health*, 12 (6): 6423–54.

Buber, M. (1923) *I and Thou* (trans. by W. Kauffman, 1970). New York: Scribners.

Buss, D.M (ed.) (2005) *The Handbook of Evolutionary Psychology*. Hoboken, NJ: Wiley Press.

Cameron, C. (2004) 'Social pedagogy and care: Danish and German practice in young people's residential care', *Journal of Social Work*, 4 (2): 133–51.

Cameron, C. (ed.) (2011) *Social Pedagogy and Working with Children and Young People: Where Care and Education Meet*. London: Jessica Kingsley.

Capaldi, C.A., Dopko, R.L. and Zelenski, J.M. (2014) 'The relationship between the nature connectedness and happiness: a meta-analysis', *Frontiers in Psychology*, 5: 976.

Caputo, J.D. (1987) *Radical Hermeneutics: Repetition, Deconstruction, and the Hermeneutic Project*. Bloomington, IN: University of Indiana Press.

Chawla, L. (1990). 'Ecstatic places': Children's environmental education, *Journal of Environmental Education*, 29 (3): 18–23.

Chawla, L. (1998) 'Significant life experiences revisited: a review of research on sources of environmental sensitivity', *Environmental Education Research*, 4: 369–82.

Chawla, L. (1999) 'Life paths into effective environmental action', *Journal of Environmental Education*, 31: 15–26.

Chawla, L. (2002) '"Spots of time": manifold ways of being in nature in childhood', in P.H. Kahn Jr and S.R. Kellert (eds), *Children and Nature: Psychology, Sociocultural and Evolutionary Investigations*, pp. 199–226. Cambridge, MA and London: MIT Press.

Chawla, L. and Cushing, D.F. (2007) 'Education for strategic environmental behaviour', *Environmental Education Research*, 13 (4): 437–52.

Chawla, L. and Derr, V. (2012) 'The development of conservation behaviours in childhood and youth', in S. Clayton (ed.), *Oxford Handbook of Environmental and Conservation Psychology*, pp. 527–55. Oxford: Oxford University Press.

Chemero, A. (2009) *Radical Embodied Cognitive Science*. Cambridge, MA: MIT Press.

Churchill, W. (1943) Speech to the House of Commons. London. Retrieved on 23 November 2018 from https://winstonchurchill.org/publications/publications-index/.

Cobb, E. (1959) *The Ecology of Imagination in Childhood*. New York: Colombia University Press.

Cohen, B. (2008) 'Introducing "The Scottish Pedagogue"', *Children in Scotland, Working It Out: Developing the Children's Sector Workforce*. Edinburgh: Children in Scotland.

Colding, J. and Barthel, S. (2017) 'An urban ecology critique on the "Smart City" model', *Journal of Clean Production*, 164: 95–101.

Davis, J.M. (2010) 'What is early childhood education for sustainability?', in J.M. Davis (ed.), *Young Children and the Environment: Early Education for Sustainability*, pp. 21–42. Cambridge: Cambridge University Press.

Davis, J. and Elliot, S. (2014) 'An orientation to early childhood education for sustainability and research – framing the text', in J. Davis and S. Elliott (eds), *Research in Early Childhood Education for Sustainability*, pp. 1–17. London: Routledge.

Deleuze, G & Guattari, F. (2004). *A Thousand Plateaus; Capitalism and Schizophrenia* (trans. by B. Massumi). London. Continuum.

Deloria, V. (1999) If you think about it, you will see that it is true, in V. Deloria, B Deloria, K. Foehner and S. Scinta (eds), *Spirit and Reason; the Vine Deloria Reader*, pp. 40–60. Golden, CO: Fulcrum Publishers.

Deloria, V. and Wildcat, D. (2001) *Power and Place: Indian Education in America*. Golden, CO: Fulcrum Publishers.

Dewey, J. (1934/1980) *Art as Experience*. New York: Perigee.

Diamond, J.M. (1987) 'Extant unless proven extinct? Or, extinct unless proven extant?', *Conservation Biology*, 1: 77–79.

Dodson, E. (2015) *Senior Professor of Philosophy: Introduction to Philosophy Lecture*. Wheaton College, USA. Retrieved on 30 December 2015 from www.wheaten.edu.

Doyle, M.E. and Smith, M.K. (1999) 'Jean-Jacques Rousseau on education', *The Encyclopaedia of Informal Education*. Retrieved on 23 May 2016 from www.infEdorg/thinkers/et-rous.htm.

Dubos, R. (1980) *The Wooing of the Earth*. London: Althone.

Elliot, S. (2013) 'Play in nature: Bush kinder in Australia', in S. Knight (ed.), *International Perspectives on Forest School: Natural Spaces to Play and Learn*, pp. 113–30. London: Sage.

Ellsworth, E. (2005) *Places of Learning: Media, Architecture, Pedagogy*. New York: Routledge Falmer.

Escobar, A. (2000) 'Culture sits in places: reflections on globalism and subaltern strategies of localization'. *Political Geography*, 20: 139–74.

European Region Action Scheme for the Mobility of University Students (ERASMUS) Project (2018) *Comparative Study of Nature-based Practice in Norway, Cheche, England*. Report and film. Retrieved on 20 December 2021 from www.naturepedagogy.com and www.livingclassrooms.org.uk.

Evans, G.W., Brauchie, G., Haq, A., Stecker, R., Wong, K. and Shapiro, E. (2007) 'Young children's environmental attitudes and behaviours', *Environmental Behaviour*, 39: 635–58.

Fägerstam, E. (2012) 'Children and young people's experience of the natural world: teachers' perceptions and observations', *Australian Journal of Environmental Education*, 28 (1): 1–16.

Figueiredo, A., Portugal, G., Sá-Couto, P. and Neto, C. (2013) 'Early learning in Portugal', in S. Knight (ed.), *International Perspectives on Forest School: Natural Spaces to Play and Learn*, pp. 65–78. London: Sage.

Foucault, M. (2005) *The Hermeneutics of the Subject* (trans. by B. Burchell), lectures at the Collège de France (1981–1982), pp. 14–16. New York: Picador.

Fox, H., Gessler, M., Higgins, A., Meade, A., Warden, C. and Williams-Ridge, S. (2021) *Environmental Kinship Framework*. Retreived on 20 December 2021 from www.environmentalkinship.org.

French, M. (1986) *Beyond Power: On Women, Men and Morals*. London: Abacus.

Friedman, H. (2008) 'Humanistic and positive psychology: The methodological and epistemological divide'. *The Humanistic Psychologist*, 36 (2): 113–26. DOI: 10.1080/08873260802111036.

Fuchs, E. (2004) 'Nature and bildung: pedagogical naturalism', in L. Daston and F. Vidal (eds), *The Moral Authority of Nature*, pp. 157–81. Chicago, IL and London: University of Chicago Press.

Gablick, S. (1993) 'Towards the ecological self', in R. Hertz (ed.) *Theories in Contemporary Art*, 2nd edn, pp. 301–9. Englewood Cliffs, NJ: Prentice Hall.

Gibson, J.J. (1979) *The Theory of Affordances*. Boston, MA: Houghton Mifflin.

Gill, T. (2012) *No Fear: Growing Up in a Risk Averse Society*. London: Calouste Gulbenkian Foundation.

Gill, T. (2014) *The Play Return: A Review of the Wider Impact of Play Initiatives*. London: Children's Play Policy Forum.

Ginsburg, J. and Audley, S. (2002) '"You don't wanna teach little kids about climate change": beliefs and barriers to sustainability education in early childhood', *International Journal of Early Childhood Environmental Education*, 7 (3): 42.

Giusti, M., Svane, U., Raymond, C. and Beery, T.H. (2018) 'A framework to assess where and how children connect to nature', *Frontiers in Psychology* (8), Article 2283. https://doi.org/10.3389/fpsyg.2017.02283

Grandisoli, E. (2013) 'Building sustainability through consumption in Brazil', in S. Knight (ed.), *International Perspectives on Forest School: Natural Spaces to Play and Learn*, pp. 79–98. London: Sage.

Greenaway, R. (1992) 'Reviewing by doing'. *Journal of Adventure Education and Outdoor Leadership*, 9 (2): 21–25.

Gundem, B. (1992) 'Vivat Comenius: A commemorative essay on Johann Amos Comenius, 1592–1670', *Journal of Curriculum and Supervision*, 8 (1): 43–55.

Gundem, B. (1998) *Understanding European Didactics – An Overview: Didactics (Didaktik, Didaktik(k), Didactique)*. Oslo: University of Oslo, Institute for Educational Research.

Gurholt, K.P. (2014) 'Joy of nature, friluftsliv education and self: Combining narrative and cultural-ecological approaches to environmental sustainability', *Journal of Adventure Education and Outdoor Learning*, 4 (3): 233–46.

Hamilton, D. (1999) 'The pedagogic paradox (or why no didactics in England?)', *Pedagogy, Culture and Society*, 7 (1): 135–52.

Haraway, D. (2016) *Staying with the Trouble: Making Kin in the Chthulucene*. Durham, NC: Duke University Press.

Harris, W.T. (2003) 'Editor's preface', in J-J. Rousseau (1892) *Emile: Or Treatise on Education* (trans. by W.H. Payne), pp. vii–xvi. New York: Prometheus Books.

Heerwagen, J.H. and Orians, G.H. (2002) 'The ecological world of children', in P.H. Kahn and S.R. Kellert (eds), *Children and Nature: Psychological, Sociocultural, and Evolutionary Investigations*, pp. 29–65. Cambridge, MA: MIT Press.

Heft, H. (1988) 'Affordances of children's environments: a functional approach to environmental description', *Children's Environment*, 5: 29–37.

Hill, A. and Brown, M. (2014) 'Intersections between place, sustainability and transformative outdoor experiences', *Journal of Adventure Education and Outdoor Learning*, 14 (3): 217–32.

Hsu, S.J. (2009) 'Significant life experiences affect environmental action: a confirmation study in eastern Taiwan', *Environmental Education Research*, 15: 497–517.

Huta, V. and Waterman, A. (2014) 'Eudaimonia and its distinction from hedonia: developing a classification and terminology for understanding conceptual and operational definitions', *Journal of Happiness Studies*, 15 (6): 1425–56.

Ingold, T. (1993) 'The temporality of the landscape: World archaeology', *Conceptions of Time and Ancient Society*, 25 (2): 152–74. Retrieved on 3 July 2012 from www.jstor.org/stable/124811.

Ingold, T. (1996) 'Human worlds are culturally constructed: against the motion', in *Key Debates in Anthropology*, pp. 112–18. London: Routledge.

Ingold, T. (2000) *The Perception of the Environment: Essays on Livelihood, Dwelling and Skill*. London and New York: Routledge.

Ingold, T. (2011) *Being Alive: Essays on Movement, Knowledge and Description*. London and New York: Routledge.

Ingold, T. (2013) *Making: Anthropology, Archaeology, Art and Architecture*. London: Routledge.

Ives, C.D., Guisti, M., Fischer, J., Abson, D.J., Christian Dorninger, K.K. and Laudan, J. (2017) 'Human-nature connection: a multidisciplinary review', *Curriculum Opinion Environmental Sustainability*, 26–27: 106–113.

Jickling, B. (2017) 'Education revisited: creating educational experiences that are held, felt and disruptive', in B. Jickling and S. Sterling (eds), *Post-Sustainability and Environmental Education: Remaking Education for the Future*, pp. 15–30. Cham, Switzerland: Palgrave Macmillan.

Jickling, B., Blenkinsop, S., Morse, M. and Jensen, A. (2018) 'Wild pedagogies: six initial touchstones for early childhood environmental educators', *Australian Journal of Environmental Education*, 34 (2): 1–13.

Jóhannesson, I.Á., Norðahl, K., Óskarsdóttir, G., Pálsdóttir, A. and Pétursdóttir, B. (2011) 'Curriculum analysis and education for sustainable development in Iceland', *Environmental Education Research*, 17 (3): 375–91.

Johnston, J.T. and Murton, B. (2007) Re/placing native science: Indigenous voices in contemporary constructions of nature. *Geographical Research*, 45 (2): 121–9.

Kahn, P.H. (2002) 'Children's affiliations with nature: structure, development, and the problem of environmental generational amnesia', in P.H. Kahn and S.R. Kellert (eds), *Children and Nature: Psychological, Sociological, and Evolutionary Investigations*, pp. 29–63. Cambridge, MA: MIT Press.

Kahn, P.H. and Kellert, S.R. (eds) (2002) *Children and Nature: Psychological, Sociological, and Evolutionary Investigations*. Cambridge, MA: MIT Press.

Kamler, B. and Thomson, P. (2006) *Helping Doctoral Students Write: Pedagogies for Supervision*. London: Routledge.

Kant, I. (1900) *Kant on Education (Uber Pedagogik)*. Boston, MA: D.C. Heath.

Keeler, R. (2008) *Natural Playscapes*. Lincoln, NE: Childcare Exchange Pub.

Kellert, S. (2012) *Birthright. People and Nature in the Modern World*. New Haven, CT: Yale University Press.

Kellert, S. and Wilson, E.O. (eds) (1993) *Biophilia Hypothesis*. Washington, DC: Island Press.

Kellert, S., Heerwagen, J. and Mador, M. (eds) (2008) *Biophillic Design: The Theory, Science, and Practice of Bringing Buildings to Life*. Hoboken, NJ: John Wiley & Sons.

Kings College, London (2011) *Understanding the diverse benefits of learning in natural environments*. Research paper. Retrieved on 25 October 2018 from http://publications.naturalengland.org.uk/publication/4524600415223808.

Kovel, J. (2002) *The Enemy of Nature: The End of Capitalism or the End of the World?* London and New York: Zed Books.

Krajnc, M.K. and Korže, A.V. (2013) 'Increasing experiential learning using eco-remediations in Slovenia', in S. Knight (ed.) *International Perspectives on Forest School: Natural Spaces to Play and Learn*. pp. 53–64. London: Sage.

Kuo, Y-C. (2010) 'Interaction, Internet Self-Efficacy, and Self-Regulated Learning as Predictors of Student Satisfaction in Distance Education Courses'. *All Graduate Theses and Dissertations*. 741.

Kyttä, M. (2003) *Children in outdoor contexts: Affordances and independent mobility in the assessment of environmental child friendliness*, PhD thesis. Centre for Urban and Regional Studies, Helsinki University of Technology.

Kyttä, M. (2006) 'Environmental child-friendliness in the light of the Bullerby model', in C. Spencer and M. Blades (eds) *Children and their Environments: Learning, Using and Designing Spaces*, pp. 141–58. Cambridge: Cambridge University Press.

Langton, M. (1996) 'What do we mean by wilderness? Wilderness and terra nullius in Australian art', *The Sydney Papers*, 8 (1): 10–31.

Larimore, R. (2016) 'Defining nature-based preschools', *International Journal of Early Childhood Environmental Education*, 4 (1): 32–6.

Larson, L.R., Green, G.T. and Castleberry, S.B. (2011) 'Construction and validation of an instrument to measure environmental orientations in a diverse group of children', *Environment and Behaviour*, 43 (1): 72–89.

Lee-Hammond, L. (2017) 'Belonging in nature, Indigenous cultures and biophilia', in T. Waller, E. Ärlemalm-Hagsér, E. B. Hansen Sandseter, L. Lee-Hammond, K. S. Lekies and S. Wyver (eds), *The SAGE Handbook of Outdoor Play and Learning*, pp. 319–33. London. Sage.

Lee-Hammond, L. and Colliver, Y. (2017) 'Indigenous methodologies in education research: case study of children's play in Soloman Islands', in T. Waller, E. Ärlemalm-Hagsér, E. B. Hansen Sandseter, L. Lee-Hammond, K. S. Lekies, S. Wyver (eds), *The SAGE Handbook of Outdoor Play and Learning*, pp. 495–511. London: Sage.

Leopold, A. (1949) *A Sand County Almanac*. Oxford: Oxford University Press.

Lewicka, M. (2011) 'Place attachment: How far have we come in the last 40 years?', *Journal of Environmental Psychology*, 31: 207–30.

Lindon, J. (2011) Too safe for their own good? *Helping Children Learn About Risk and Life Skills*. London: National Early Years Network/NCB.

Little, H. and Eager, D. (2010) 'Risk, challenge and safety: implications for play quality and playground design', *European Early Childhood Education Research Journal*, 18 (4): 487–513.

Little, H., Sandseter, E.B. and Wyver, S. (2012) 'Early childhood teachers' beliefs about children's risky play in Australia and Norway', *Contemporary Issues in Early Childhood*, 13 (4): 300–16.

Little Bear, L. (2000) 'Jagged world views colliding', in M. Battise (ed.), *Reclaiming Indigenous Voice and Vision*, pp. 77–85. Vancouver: UBC Press.

Longenecker, R.N. (1982) 'The pedagogical nature of the law in *Galatians* 3:19–4:17'. *Journal of the Evangelical Theological Society*, 25 (1): 53–61.

Lorenz, S. (1994) 'Book Reviews'. *School Psychology International*, 15 (4): 379. https://doi.org/10.1177/0143034394154014

Louv, R. (2005) *Last Child in the Woods*. Chapel Hill, NC: Algonquin Books.

MacFarlane, R. (2017) *The Wild Spaces*. London: Granta Books.

MacQuarrie, S., Nugent, C. and Warden, C. (2015) 'Learning with nature and learning from others: nature as setting and resource for early childhood education', *Journal of Adventure Education and Outdoor Learning*, 15 (1): 1–23.

Martin, K. (2003) 'Ways of knowing, being and doing: A theoretical framework and methods for Indigenous and indigenist re-search', *Journal of Australian Studies*, 27 (76): 203–14.

Mawson, W.B. (2014) 'Experiencing the "wild woods": the impact of pedagogy on children's experience of a natural environment', *European Early Childhood Education Research Journal*. DOI: 10.1080/1350293X.2014.947833.

Merindah (2017) *Australian Geographic* website. Comment on news article by *STAFF*. Retrieved on 20 April 2017 from https://www.australiangeographic.com.au/.

Miller, G.T.M and Spoolman, S.E. (2013) *Environmental Science* (14th edition). Belmont, CA: Brookes/Cole.

Mitchell, R. (2013) 'Is physical activity in natural environments better for mental health than physical activity in other environments?', *Social Science & Medicine*, 91: 130–4.

Moss, S. (2012) *Natural Childhood*. National Trust Report, PDF version 2. Retrieved on 20 December 2021 from https://nt.global.ssl.fastly.net/documents/read-our-natural-childhood-report.pdf.

Muir, J. (1988) *John Muir in His own Words: A Book of Quotations*, in P. Browning (ed.). Lafayette, CA: Great West.

Munn, N. (2014) 'We don't need a map: a Martu experience of the Western Desert', in K. Mahood (ed.), p. 146. Exhibition Book.

Naess, A. (1973) 'The shallow and the deep, long range ecology movement', *Inquiry*, 16.

Nature Action Collaborative for Children (NACC) (2008) *Re-connecting the World's Children to Nature*. Paper presented at the Working Forum on Nature Education: New tools for Connecting the World's Children with Nature. Nebraska City,

Nebraska, USA. Retrieved from www.worldforumfoundation.org on 22 January 2018. Call to action pdf written by global advisors, including C. Warden.

Nazam, F. and Husain, A. (2016) 'Exploring spiritual values among school children', *International Journal of School Cognitive Psychology*, 3 (2). DOI: 10.4172/2469-9837.1000175.

Nelson, R.K. (1983) *Make Prayers to the Raven: A Koyukon View of the Northern Forest*. Chicago, IL: University of Chicago Press.

Nicholson, S. (1977) 'How not to cheat the children: the theory of loose parts', *Landscape Architecture Quarterly*, 62 (1): 30–4.

Nutti, Y.J. (2017) 'Along paths of movement: Sami children and early childhood student teachers as Wayfarers', in T. Waller, E. Ärlemalm-Hagsér, E. B. Hansen Sandseter, L. Lee-Hammond, K. S. Lekies, S. Wyver (eds), *The SAGE Handbook of Outdoor Play and Learning*, pp. 333–48. London: Sage.

Oliver, S. (2005) *Philosophy, God and Motion*. London: Radical Orthodoxy, Routledge.

Oliver, K. (2009) *Animal Lessons: How They Teach Us to be Human*. New York: Columbia University Press.

Ollin, R. (2008) 'Silent pedagogy and rethinking classroom practice: structuring teaching through silence rather than talk', *Cambridge Journal of Education*, 38 (2): 265–80. DOI: 10.1080/03057640802063528.

Oxford English Dictionary (2018) *Pedagogy*. Retrieved on 23 April 2018 from https://www.oed.com/viewdictionaryentry/Entry/139520.

Papatheodorou, T. (2013) 'The veggie bag and its potential for connected knowing in South Africa', in S. Knight (ed.), *International Perspectives on Forest School: Natural Spaces to Play and Learn*, pp. 99–112. London: Sage.

Perrin, J.L. and Benassi, V.A. (2009) 'The connectedness to nature scale: A measure of emotional connection to nature?', *Journal of Environmental Pyschology*, 29 (4). pp. 434–40.

Pipher, M. (2008) *The Shelter of Each Other*. New York: Riverhead Books.

Plumwood, V. (2003) 'Decolonizing relationships with nature', in W.M. Adams and M. Mulligan (eds), *Decolonizing Nature: Strategies for Conservation in a Post-Colonial Era*, pp. 51–78. London: Earthscan.

Raymond, C.M, Giusti, M. and Barthel, S. (2017) 'An embodied perspective on the co-production of cultural ecosystem services: Toward embodied ecosystems', *Journal of Environmental Planning and Management*, 61: 1–22.

Richardson, M., Cormack, A., McRobert, L. and Underhill, R. (2016) '30 days wild: Development and evaluation of a large-scale nature engagement campaign to improve well-being', *PLoS ONE*, 11 (2): e0149777. doi:10.1371/journal. pone.0149777.

Rickinson, M. (2001) 'Learners and learning in environmental education: a critical review of the evidence' (special issue), *Environmental Education Research*, 7 (3): 208–320 (whole issue).

Roberts, M. and Wills, P.R. (1998) 'Understanding Maori epistemology: a scientific perspective', in H. Wautischer (ed.), *Tribal Epistemologies: Essays in the Philosophy of Anthropology*, pp. 43–77. Brookfield, WI and Aldershot: Ashgate.

Roberts, M., Haami B., Benton, R., Satterfield, T., Finucane, M., Henare, M. and
    Henare, M. (2004) 'Whakapapa as a Maori mental construct: some implications
    for the debate over genetic modification of organisms', *The Contemporary
    Pacific*, 16. DOI: 10.1353/cp.2004.0026.
Robinson, E. (1977) *The Original Vision: A Study of Religious Experience in
    Childhood*. Oxford: Religious Experience Research Centre.
Rockefeller, S. and Elder, J.C. (eds) (1992) *Spirit and Nature: Why the
    Environment Is a Religious Issue*. Boston, MA: Beacon Press.
Roe, J. and Aspinall, P. (2011) 'The emotional affordances of forest settings:
    an investigation in boys with extreme behavioural problems', *Journal of
    Landscape and Research*, 36 (5): 535–552.
Rolston, H. (1986) *Philosophy Gone Wild*. Buffalo, NY: Prometheus.
Rosa, C.D., Profice, C.C. and Collado, S. (2018) 'Nature experiences and adults'
    self-reported pro-environmental behaviours: the role of connectedness to
    nature and childhood nature experiences', *Frontiers in Psychology*, 9: 1055.
    DOI: 10.3389/fpsyg.2018.01055.
Rowan, M.C. (2017) 'Relating with land/engaging with elders: accessing
    Indigenous knowledges in early education through outdoor encounters', in
    T. Waller, E. Ärlemalm-Hagsér, E.B. Hansen Sandseter, L. Lee-Hammond,
    K. Lekies and S. Wyver (eds), *The SAGE Handbook of Outdoor Play and
    Learning*, pp. 395–413. London: Sage.
Rousseau, J-J. (1762/2003) *Emile: Or Treatise on Education* (trans. by W.H.
    Payne). New York: Prometheus Books.
Sandell, K. and Öhman, J. (2013) 'An educational tool for outdoor education
    and environmental concern', *Journal of Adventure Education and Outdoor
    Learning*, 13 (1): 36–55.
Sandseter, E.B. (2009) 'Characteristics of risky play', *Journal of Adventure
    Education and Outdoor Learning*, 9 (1): 3–21.
Sandseter, E.B. (2012) 'Restrictive safety or unsafe freedom? Norwegian ECEC
    practitioners' perceptions and practices concerning children's risky play',
    Childcare in Practice, 18 (1): 83–101.
Schmidtz, D. and Williot, E. (2002) 'Reinventing the Commons: An African
    Case Study', *U.C. Davis Law Review*, 37 (203): 203–52. Retrieved on 20
    December 2021 from https://environs.law.ucdavis.edu/volumes/27/1/schmidtz_
    willott.pdf.
Sideris, L. (2017) *Consecrating Science*. Berkeley, CA: University of California
    Press.
Smith, M.K. (2009) 'Social pedagogy', *Encyclopaedia of Informal Education*.
    Retrieved on 1 May 2017 from https://infed.org/mobi/social-pedagogy/.
Sobel, D. (2008) *Childhood and Nature: Design Principles for Education*.
    Portland, ME: Stenhouse Publishers.
Spence, M.D. (1999) *Dispossessing the Wilderness: Indian Removal and the
    Making of the National Park*. New York: Oxford Press.
Steinbeck, J. (1941) *Log from the Sea of Cortez*. Mamaroneck, NY: Appel.
Szczepanski, A. and Dahlgren, L.O. (2011) 'Teachers' perspectives of learning
    outdoors'. *Didaktisk Tidskrift*, 20 (2): 119–44.

Tafoya, T. (1995) 'Finding harmony: Balancing traditional values with Western science in therapy', *Canadian Journal of Native Education*, 21: 7–27.

Taylor, A. (2011) Reconceptualizing the 'nature' of childhood. *Childhood*. 18 (4): 420–33.

Taylor, A. (2013) *Reconfiguring the Natures of Childhood* (Contesting Early Childhood series). Abingdon: Routledge.

Taylor, A. (2017) 'Beyond stewardship: common world pedagogies for the Anthropocene', *Environmental Education Research*, 23 (1): 1448–61.

Taylor, A. and Pacini-Ketchbaw, V. (2015) 'Learning with children, ants and worms in the Anthropocene: towards a common world pedagogy of multispecies vulnerability', *Pedagogy, Culture and Society*, 23 (4): 507–29.

Taylor, B. (2009). *Dark Green Religion: Nature, Spirituality, and the Planetary Future*. Berkeley, CA: University of California Press.

Te Urewara Act (2014) New Zealand legislation. Retrieved on 1 October 2018 from www.legislation. govt.nz/act/public/2014/0051/latest/DLM6183601.html.

Tobin, J., Hseuh, Y. and Karasawa, M. (2009) *Preschool in Three Cultures Revisited: China, Japan, and the United States*. Chicago, IL: University of Chicago Press.

Tovey, H. (2007) *Playing Outdoors*. Maidenhead: Open University Press.

Tucker, M.E. (2002) 'Religion and ecology: the interaction of cosmology and cultivation', in S. Kellert and T. Farnham (eds), *The Good in Nature and Humanity: Connecting Science, Religion and Spirituality with the Natural World*, pp. 61–90. Washington, DC: Island Press.

Uhrmacher, B. (1995) 'Uncommon schooling: a historical look at Rudolf Steiner, anthroposophy and Waldorf education', *Curriculum Inquiry*, 25 (4): 381–406. Ontario: Blackwell.

United Nations. (1982) *World Charter for Nature*. Retrieved on 25 January 2018 from http://www.un.org/documents/ga/res/37/a37r007.htm

United Nations (1990) *UN Convention on the Rights of the Child*. United Nations. Retrieved on 10 March 2022 from https://www.unicef.org.uk/what-we-do/un-convention-child-rights/.

United Nations (2015) *Sustainable Development Goals*. Retrieved on 25 January 2018 from www.un.org/sustainabledevelopment/sustainable-development-goals/.

Waite, S. and Pratt, N. (2011) 'Theoretical perspectives on learning outside the classroom – relationships between learning and place, in S. Waite (ed.), *Learning Outside the Classroom: From Birth to Eleven*, pp. 1–18. London: Sage.

Waite, S., Passy, R., Gilchrist, M., Hunt, A. and Blackwell, I. (2016) *Natural Connections Demonstration Project, 2012–2016: Final Report*. Natural England Commissioned Reports, number 215.

Waite, S., Rogers, S. and Evans, J. (2013) 'Freedom, flow and fairness: exploring how children develop socially at school through outdoor play', *Journal of Adventure Education and Outdoor Learning*, 13 (3): 255–76.

Waller, T., Ärlemalm-Hagsér, E., Hansen Sandseter, E.B., Lee-Hammond, L., Lekies, K. and Wyver, S. (eds) (2017) *The SAGE Handbook of Outdoor Play and Learning*. London: Sage.

Waller, T. and Tovey, H. (2014) 'Outdoor play and learning', in T. Waller and G. Davis (eds), *An Introduction to Early Childhood: A Multidisciplinary Approach*, pp. 146–65. London: Sage.

Warden, C. (1996) *Talking and Thinking Floorbooks*. Scotland: Mindstretchers.

Warden, C. (2007) *Nurture through Nature: Working with Children Under Three in Nature*. Scotland: Mindstretchers.

Warden, C. (2010) *Nature Kindergartens and Forest Schools: An Exploration of Naturalistic Learning within Nature Kindergartens and Forest Schools*. Scotland: Mindstretchers.

Warden, C. (2015) *Learning with Nature – Embedding Outdoor Practice*. London: Sage.

Warden, C. (2017) 'Nature pedagogy – An exploration of the storied narratives that illustrate its application across spaces inside, outside and beyond', in T. Waller, E. Ärlemalm-Hagsér, E.B. Hansen Sandseter, L. Lee-Hammond, K. Lekies and S. Wyver (eds), *The SAGE Handbook of Outdoor Play and Learning*, pp. 279–95. London: Sage.

Warden, C. (2018) *Nature Pedagogy: A Common Thread Connecting Nature-based Settings Worldwide*. Washington, DC: Natural Start Alliance.

Waters, J. and Maynard, T. (2010) What's so interesting about outside? A study of child-initiated interaction with teachers in the natural outdoor environment. *European Early Childhood Research Journal*, 18 (4): 473–83.

Wells, N. and Lekies, K. (2006) 'Nature and the life course: pathways from childhood nature experiences to adult environmentalism', *Children, Youth and Environments*, 16 (1): 1–24.

Whitescarver, K. and Cossentino, J. (2008) 'Montessori and the mainstream: a century of reform on the margins', *Teachers College Record*, 110 (12): 2571–600.

Wildman, W.J. (2006) *Relational Ontology*. Retrieved on 18 December 2017 from https://bit.ly/2Sejq4D.

Wilson, E.O. (1997) *In Search of Nature*. Washington, DC: Island Press.

Wilson, R. (2020) Personal correspondence.

Wolsko, C. and Lindberg, K. (2013) 'Experiencing connection with nature: the matrix of psychological well-being, mindfulness and outdoor recreation', *Ecopsychology*, 5 (2): 80–91.

Yeh, H.P., Stone, J.A., Churchill, S.M., Wheat, J.S., Brymer, E. and Davids, K. (2015) 'Physical, psychological and emotional benefits of green physical activity: an ecological dynamics perspective', *Sports Medicine*, 46 (7): 947–53.

Index